DARK THOUGHTS

———

ON WRITING

Also by Stanley Wiater

NIGHT VISIONS 7 (1989) (editor)

DARK DREAMERS: CONVERSATIONS WITH THE MASTERS OF HORROR (1990)

THE OFFICIAL TEENAGE MUTANT NINJA TURTLES TREASURY (1991)

DARK VISIONS: CONVERSATIONS WITH THE MASTERS OF THE HORROR FILM (1992)

AFTER THE DARKNESS (1993) (editor)

COMIC BOOK REBELS: CONVERSATIONS WITH THE CREATORS OF THE NEW COMICS (co-authored with Stephen R. Bissette) (1993)

DARK THOUGHTS

ON WRITING

Advice and Commentary
from Fifty
Masters of Fear and Suspense

STANLEY WIATER

Underwood Books
Grass Valley
1997

DARK THOUGHTS: ON WRITING

ISBN 1-887424-30-X (trade paper)

An Underwood Books title by arrangement with the author. No part of this book may be reproduced in any form or by any electronic or mechanical means including information storage and retrieval systems without explicit permission from the author or the author's agent, except by a reviewer who may quote brief passages. For information address the publisher: Underwood Books, PO Box 1609, Grass Valley, California 95945. The author can be reached via email at: StanWiater@aol.com

Distributed by Publisher's Group West

Manufactured in the United States of America

Cover design by Nora Wertz. Background graphic by Virgil Finlay

10 9 8 7 6 5 4 3 2 1

First Edition

Beyond their original newspaper or magazine appearances, portions of the material collected herein was previously published in the books DARK DREAMERS: CONVERSATIONS WITH THE MASTERS OF HORROR (Avon Books, 1990), DARK VISIONS: CONVERSATIONS WITH THE MASTERS OF THE HORROR FILM (Avon Books, 1992), and COMIC BOOK REBELS: CONVERSATIONS WITH THE CREATORS OF THE NEW COMICS, co-authored with Stephen R. Bissette (Donald I. Fine, 1993). Other material collected herein, including author quotes, is previously unpublished. All quotes appearing in chapters are selected from exclusive interviews conducted with the author.

Library of Congress Cataloging-in-Publication Data:

Dark thoughts: on writing: advice and commentary from the masters of fear and suspense / [compiled by] Stanley Wiater. –1st ed.

p. cm

Includes bibliographical references.

ISBN 1-887424-30-X

1. Horror tales--Authorship. 2. Science fiction--Authorship. 3. Authors--Interviews. I.Wiater, Stan.

PN3377.5.H67D37 1997

808.3'8738–dc21   97-26743

CIP

To Ray Bradbury
for showing me the way to
The October Country
and inspiring me to join
The Autumn People.

ACKNOWLEDGEMENTS

First and foremost, a sincere and heartfelt "thank you" to all the authors, artists, and filmmakers who have been kind enough to sit down with me through the years and answer my endless questions. (And for some of you, to quote an already overused movie line: "I'll be back.")

A major tip of the hat to Tim Underwood, whose remarks while discussing an entirely different project brought this volume forth, fully alive and kicking, practically overnight.

My thanks to Dan Berger, Stephen Murphy, A.C. Farley, Peter Laird, Jeannine Atkins, George R. Ledoux, Linda Wiater, Roger Anker, Michael Brewer, Michele Wiater for services and support above and beyond the call.

To Candida Fernandez and Braulio Arroyo for their unshakable faith and support.

Finally, my deepest thanks as always to Iris and Tanya, whose beaming smiles are bright enough to guide me back from the edge of darkness. (Not to mention the damnable abyss of zero hour computer glitches.)

S.W.

CONTRIBUTORS

Clive Barker
Stephen R. Bissette
Robert Bloch
Ray Bradbury
Gary Brandner
Ramsey Campbell
John Carpenter
Joseph A. Citro
Larry Cohen
Nancy A. Collins
Matthew J. Costello
Wes Craven
David Cronenberg
Les Daniels
Dennis Etchison
John Farris
Neil Gaiman
Ed Gorman
Charles L. Grant
Rick Hautala
James Herbert
Jack Ketchum
Stephen King
Dean Koontz
Joe R. Lansdale
Richard Laymon

Edward Lee
Fritz Leiber
Ira Levin
Graham Masterton
Richard Matheson
Richard Christian Matheson
Robert R. McCammon
Michael McDowell
Frank Miller
Thomas F. Monteleone
Alan Moore
David Morrell
William F. Nolan
Anne Rice
George A. Romero
John Russo
John Saul
David J. Schow
Joseph Stefano
Peter Straub
Whitley Strieber
Thomas Tessier
Chet Williamson
J.N. Williamson
F. Paul Wilson
Gahan Wilson

TABLE OF CONTENTS

If a way to the better there be, it lies in taking a full look at the worst.
—Thomas Hardy

This thing of darkness I acknowledge mine.
—William Shakespeare

A pearl of wisdom remains luminous regardless of age or owner.
—Edgar D. Pynchon

INTRODUCTION

This may not be the wisest confession to make after all these years, but I've always had a "hidden agenda" in my dual literary career as a journalist and a writer of dark fiction.

You see, although I've enjoyed great professional satisfaction profiling the major creative talents in the overlapping genres of horror and dark suspense, I actually broke into the business of non-fiction because I've always been, well, a sort of psychic vampire at heart. . . . Or do I reveal too much already to those swallowing the stereotype that you must be certifiably "warped" to be appreciative of the dark side of life or the arts?

All I'm trying to say is, although I've been a free-lance journalist since 1975, I originally intended to be solely a fiction writer. Like so many others represented here, I was "twisted" at an early age by the classic works of Edgar Allan Poe and H.P. Lovecraft, and knew I had to follow, however awkwardly, in their awe-inspiring, life-changing, exquisitely monstrous footsteps.

So when an opportunity presented itself in 1974 (while studying the Hollywood film industry for a summer on a college scholarship) to meet my favorite writer, Ray Bradbury, how could I *not* ignore making the most of this marvelous, possibly once-in-a-lifetime, encounter? The problem was, how to present myself to this world-famous author as a hip young professional—not a gawking, all but incoherent fan who was also hoping to somehow glean a few precious "writer's secrets" from him?

Very simple solution: I instantly became a "reporter-at-large" for a weekly newspaper back in Massachusetts—before their editors ever knew I even existed. Armed with this paper-thin disguise, I ultimately did spend an unforgettable evening with Bradbury at his home. (And then subsequently sold the interview to that very same newspaper, in a clear case of going back to the future.) Although it would be six more years before I sold my first piece of fiction (in a short story competition judged by some obscure writer named Stephen King), I could truthfully declare myself a more than capable interviewer. And one already possessed of an unusually keen appreciation and special insight into this often misdiagnosed area of literature and popular culture.

With such a modest assessment of my skills, I embarked on my initial literary career as an "arts & entertainment reporter" and critic. Of course, what I *really* had was a legitimate opportunity to meet my favorite writers, artists, and filmmakers. And the chance to learn, first-hand, each and every one of their creative secrets.

So that's where the "psychic vampire" analogy comes in to play: if I could present myself as an unusually dedicated journalist, perhaps I could then quench my unending thirst for the secrets of creating truly memorable dark fiction. Fortunately, my interest was doubly sincere—not only did I truly love and respect this "fiction of fear" as a reader, but I deeply desired to write professionally. Why not learn at the mouth of the masters, so to speak?

In a way, this lifelong devotion was my secret weapon—my creative edge in terms of getting these wonderfully creative people to tell me tales they might not reveal to just another disinterested, assignment-for-the-day reporter. What better interviewer could a subject have than someone who'd proudly declare: "You don't have to worry about being portrayed foolishly or unfeelingly in this interview. I've read every one of your books—or seen all of your movies. And, by the way, I've most likely read all the books of your favorite author, too."

So back in the late Seventies I began to live out the cliché of becoming just what I had always pretended to be. Not only did I have a viable career profiling our greatest authors and screenwriters; but by quietly searching and politely probing, I might also learn *directly from them just how they "did it."* Just how they were able to scare and thrill their audiences to the maximum degree. How they were able to repeatedly face up to their fears, to look again and again directly into the abyss without ever falling into it themselves. To find out just what made them "tick" so perhaps, along the way, I might somehow also discover what made me "tick" as well.

So even if the magazine or newspaper I was working for at the time was interested only in the celebrity's latest bestseller or movie deal, I made it a point to sneak in a few technical questions—fully aware they were not of interest to the general public. (Of course, the golden assignments were when the piece was intended for a publication like *Writer's Digest*. Then I had absolutely no hesitation in demanding the subject at hand reveal their closely guarded secrets and techniques.) Only I knew these questions would be of considerable value to anyone interested in being a professional writer themselves one day. Okay—even if that subject's comments never saw the light of publication, their candid advice and personal insights were sure as hell of intense interest to at least *one* fledgling author.

Which is how *Dark Thoughts: On Writing* came into being: one writer, one quote, at a time. Having had the immense pleasure of meeting practically every major horror and dark suspense writer published in the past quarter century, it seemed only natural that a quotebook dealing with this topic might prove of value to others. And so, after diligently checking back through all my interviews and profiles (including a few inadvertently unpublished), I've attempted to capture here—from more than fifty universally acknowledged masters of their craft—the essence of their creative "dark thoughts." (Along with several screenwriters who are even better known to the public as directors of horror or suspense films.)

The general categories which follow really need no further elaboration—with maybe the exception of the final one. "*Where do get your ideas?*" has supposedly always been the most difficult (and sometimes most ridiculous) question for any writer to effectively answer a demanding fan or interviewer.

However, beyond the times I posed this very question in a standard interview, the query was made on a more formal basis in my two anthologies of original fiction, *Night Visions 7* (1989) and *After The Darkness* (1993). In each volume I asked every contributor to take work-in-progress notes so as to later explain just when and why and how they created their particular (and in most cases *very* particular) short story. A sampling of these self-termed "after-words" is included here. They offer a fascinating glimpse of how a professional writer can drop a random idea or two into a top hat and then somehow make a magnificent flock of ravens take sudden flight from it.

The appendices are intended for both potential writers and scholars of the field. The first, "A Reader's Guide To Writing Horror" will give the reader a thorough grounding—and this title may be even more appropriate—in "Everything You Ever Wanted to Know about Writing

Horror But Were Afraid to Ask." From reference books, writers organizations, trade newsletters, magazines, to horror author websites on the Internet, it's all there to help "twist" you in the right direction.

To investigate the art of darkness as literature, "Modern Horror Fiction: A Selection of the 113 Best," is my choice of the 113 books (with a bonus listing of the best anthologies) one must be familiar with before ever attempting to further this truly great literary tradition.

So, please, come this way. Don't worry—all your questions will be answered. That and even more than you had previously dared to imagine.

Watch your head. This way— it's not that much further down, I assure you. Enter my private library, amassed from a lifetime of reading and collecting the very best— as recommended to yours truly by the very best. Feel free to browse around. Have a long drink at a particular novel . . . or just a few sips at a short story or two. Don't be afraid to be a "vampire" too if you also share an unquenchable thirst for knowledge and practical advice from those who do it so well their pages practically bleed.

You have absolutely nothing to fear.

Except for maybe for the tall stranger coming up unexpectedly from behind because he believes this book you're reading is somehow actually about him. About his secret madness at pretending to be a mild-mannered reader, when actually he's the most obsessed and frightening of new writers.

Who will go to any lengths to prevent his being revealed to anyone who dares to look for him between these covers. Better stop now, better turn and confront him before it's too late.

Put down the book. Now! While you still can, damn it!

Don't you hear that heavy breathing?

For God's sake, look behind you! Someone's right over your—

Made you look, didn't I?

Ahhh . . . just one of the many, many glorious secrets to be entertained and appreciated in these *Dark Thoughts: On Writing.*

Stanley Wiater
Deerfield, Massachusetts
May 14, 1997

CHAPTER ONE

Basic Influences

[I'm fascinated by writers] because I learned from them, and I loved them. I don't understand writers who are not madly in love with other writers. I'm a library person. I never made it to college, so I educated myself at the library. I spent days in there, and months, and years. At least twice a week for ten years—from the time I was 18 till I was 28—educating myself all by books. Reading in every section of the library—over in philosophy, in history, in essays, in poetry—you name it! So therefore the library is my home. That's where I was born!

And my love for certain authors is so immense—I carry Shaw with me wherever I go, I carry Shakespeare. Alexander Pope. I go back and reread the great writers because they teach you, they're really superb. We have really very few writers alive today that are as good as they are.
RAY BRADBURY

There's a handful of writers whose influence on me has been greater than anyone else's. So I tend to keep their books nearby: John D. MacDonald, James M. Cain, Ray Bradbury, Charles Dickens, several others. I'll sometimes start the morning by picking up one of their books, a particular favorite, and read a few paragraphs at random to appreciate the use of language. Writers I tend to use this way had a terrific sense of the language, and could write a sentence that really moved, that had a dazzling shine to it. I'll say, "Damn, that's good!" and it motivates me to want to do something that might approach the imagery and musicality of prose that I admire in them.
DEAN KOONTZ

I'm extremely lucky. When I was very young, I wanted to be a priest. But in sixth grade, I read my first Ray Bradbury story and then I wanted to be a writer and I've never once changed my mind since. Now, I'm able to a make a living writing. And so is my wife. For all the ups and downs, and occasional heartbreaks, we know how lucky we are to be able to do what we really love. God has blessed us, no doubt about it, and I realize this particularly when I get letters from my readers and see that I'm able to entertain them from time to time. As I said, I'm extremely lucky.

ED GORMAN

With the exception of Ray Bradbury, I can't honestly say I was "influenced" by anybody as much as I just liked to *read*. People may say "I was influenced by this writer and I was influenced by that writer," but I believe horror writers are really influenced most of all by their childhoods. I wonder if most horror writers had happy childhoods. I wonder if things have happened that made us this way— it seems like we're always trying to get back to our childhood. Trying to find something we lost, or correct something we missed. Or purge it.

ROBERT R. McCAMMON

I remember sitting there, just going through the table of contents for Ray Bradbury's *The October Country* for the first time. Just reading the titles of a lot of those stories was enough to give me shivers! "The Cistern," "The Jar," "The Next in Line," "The Wind," "The Scythe." Just the *titles* were so evocative! It wasn't so much the images they brought to mind, but the expectations—my God, what can *that* be about?

THOMAS F. MONTELEONE

When I was ten I read "An Occurrence at Owl Creek Bridge" by Ambrose Bierce. *That* had a powerful effect on me.

When I was eleven, I began reading Ray Bradbury, which produced an incomparable, life-changing result. And Bradbury lead me into reading Richard Matheson, Charles Beaumont, A.E. Van Vogt, and a number of wonderful science fiction writers. Of course those were the 1950's, when science fiction was happening.

DENNIS ETCHISON

First there were the monster magazines and the horror movies when I was a teenager. Then, when I got into college, I read a lot of fantasy: J.R.R. Tolkien, and Howard's Conan, and a lot of the William Morris-type of story. I even read Thongor novels, God help me. I read so much of it I overdosed, and I find I can't read fantasy any more. But I didn't read the real masters of horror—M.R. James, Algernon Blackwood—until after I was out of college. Again, only if it was reprinted in paperback, though I started buying the Arkham House books when I was in college, and kept that up. In fact, I was looking at them the other day, and found I only need about twenty-five more to complete my collection.

CHET WILLIAMSON

Besides Poe and Lovecraft, I read Ambrose Bierce early on. *The Damned Thing and Other Stories.* He had a very special talent, which I feel is a real help—if not a requirement—for writing horror or dark suspense. He possessed a very sardonic wit, a real sharp sense of sarcasm. His cynical view of the world came through in all his short stories. They were wonderfully acerbic.

THOMAS F. MONTELEONE

Before I wrote *The Vampire Lestat,* one of the things that made me return to the genre was reading Stephen King and Peter Straub and seeing what they were able to do. I wanted to get back in there and "outdo" them! It's a wonderful desire! I also read a lot of the great English horror writers, like M.R. James, J. Sheridan LeFanu, and Algernon Blackwood. Blackwood is a very erotic and wonderful horror writer.

ANNE RICE

I always loved Richard Matheson's work. The way he touched on horror and science fiction, and then would mix the two with a certain subtlety.

F. PAUL WILSON

I was one of those who didn't read horror. I only saw one horror movie when I was a kid that I can recall, and that was the original *The Thing.* I remember it gave me nightmares for *days* afterwards. The next horror movie I saw was as a teenager when *Psycho* came out, and I was eighteen. I wished I hadn't—it was a long time before I could use a tub-shower again.

JOHN SAUL

My mother gave me *Peter Pan* and a few other fantasies such as *Wind in the Willows* when I was a kid, but they were benign volumes. It was only through my own pursuits that I came upon the darker stuff, like Poe. But I am not, nor have I ever been, the sort of person who thought that dark fantasy—horror fiction—would be my sole preoccupation. In the fullness of my career—supposing I continue to work another thirty or forty years—I think it will be perceived to be an element of my work, but by no means the dominant element. My parents always knew I was imaginative. I think they always *worried* about that. I don't believe they ever put pen and paper into my hands and said, "Get on with it" or "Write whatever your imagination directs you." Far from it! I think they had the conventional belief of making sure that I somehow found a purpose in life which would pay the mortgage and allow me to be a sane and productive member of society. So they let me get on with my interests, but they certainly didn't encourage them.

CLIVE BARKER

Discovering H.P. Lovecraft was for me—like I suppose it is for a lot of horror writers—a key moment in my life. The paperback editions of *The Colour Out of Space* and Others, and *The Dunwich Horror* and Others, and *The Case of Charles Dexter Ward*. They were really formidable influences. My favorite Lovecraft story, which continues to rule my life, is "At the Mountains of Madness." This idea of taking this white, frozen landscape and turning it into a "horror house"—it was the antithesis of the creepy, old house. And in such an exotic, foreign location! Years later, I basically ended up doing my own "Cthulhu Mythos" novel which used as a jumping point an Antarctic location—that was *Midsummer*.

MATTHEW J. COSTELLO

I'm sure this is a familiar refrain, but Poe's work really did strike me as being so wonderful that I couldn't wait to get to the next story. I remember feeling the same way about Ambrose Bierce and H.P. Lovecraft. They all had a strong effect on my early years.

DAVID MORRELL

I read *all* of H.P. Lovecraft, and that was very influential. I get from him reliance on a landscape. A sense of place; that comes directly from him. I've read a lot of horror and occult short stories.

Other influences would be mostly Chinese and Japanese films of the occult. Not for anything specific, but just for their way of treating the supernatural in a straightforward fashion in a way that Americans never quite get. As a part of life. And they are simply telling a story in which the supernatural is a major element. I still go to see all the Chinese horror films I can. Number one, because I enjoy them.

Number two, because you can steal from them!
MICHAEL MCDOWELL

Virtually every decent piece of fiction I read teaches me something I didn't know. A few of those writers whose work I've consciously studied and, to some degree, imitated: Hemingway, Fitzgerald, Nathaniel West, John D. McDonald, Chester Himes, Dean Koontz, Stephen King, Peter Rabe, Ed McBain, Bill Pronzini, Evan Connell, Charles Bukowski, Max Allan Collins, Marcia Muller, Ross McDonald, Dorothy B. Hughes, Richard Matheson, and most certainly Robert Bloch.
ED GORMAN

I'm old enough to have caught the end of the radio era, in terms of dramatic shows: *The Shadow, Inner Sanctum, Suspense.* I still collect old radio shows on tape and record because they were an influence on me. But I also read horror comics, of course, as most kids were during the Fifties. And I was very impressed by the E.C. Comics— *Tales from the Crypt, Vault of Horror, The Haunt of Fear.* Everybody says they were influenced by them now so that it's a cliché.... Strangely enough, my father—who always gave me a moderately hard time about the fact that I was morbidly interested in all this—used to introduce me to a lot of books in the field. My mother gave me a copy of Lovecraft's *The Outsider* as a high school graduation gift. I don't know how to explain this, even now.
LES DANIELS

Oh, Lovecraft has been an *enormous* influence. I really admire very much what he did—he actually blasted the division between fantasy and science fiction. He really messed it up, and he did it by means of writing horror his own particular way.
GAHAN WILSON

There is a certain glee in my work, I'll admit. But for me, it heightens the horror. It's really a little trick I learned from Robert

Bloch. I think my approach and style is very different than Bloch's, but he is really the one who taught me—and so many others—that horror and humor are opposite sides of the sword. When I was growing up, Bloch was undoubtedly my favorite horror writer—and is still—one of my favorite horror writers. Maybe the favorite horror writer of them all. The hard-boiled mystery writers influenced me in terms of style and approach. In many ways, I consider Robert Bloch a hard-boiled writer, with *Psycho* and *The Scarf*. Those are masterpieces. I think the hard-boiled voice has influenced me a lot more than horror writers. In the same way, Flannery O'Connner has been an enormous influence. So I like that straight-forward, here it is, "fuck you" attitude. Bloch gave me an attitude. And I always liked that posture, because if I was going to read horror, I wanted it to be scary. For me, he *was* scarier that way. I think there's nothing more frightening than to find horrible things somewhat amusing.

JOE R. LANSDALE

Robert Aickman, for a start [still scares me]. Stories that he wrote have stayed with me for days; he is the writer in the field who I most reread. I'm always learning something new the next time around. But Stephen King, of course—I'll always remember that scene in Room 217 in *The Shining*. And Peter Straub. Or Fritz Leiber, who often still instills that sense of awe in me. I suppose I look for that more than anything else in a writer.

RAMSEY CAMPBELL

Ever since I discovered John Farris I haven't found any author writing scary work for a longer time, or who does it better than he does. He's at the top of the field, as far as sheer writing ability goes. He just dazzles me! When he's on, nobody comes close. He's simultaneously in the field, but not trapped by it, know what I mean? When he was still a teenager, I think he wrote something like four novels under pseudonyms. I remember the first copy of *Harrison High* that I got (which was successful enough to warrant several sequels) had a picture on the back cover of John when he was age 23. And I'm thinking, "Jesus, when I was 23, [as a writer] I didn't know my left from my right." I had just published my first short story, and here I was staring at a guy who, to my mind, had all the answers.

DAVID J. SCHOW

Oh, Ray Bradbury influenced all of us—there's no doubt of that! I had sold only two short stories at the time I wrote him. And he answered, and was very gracious, and very helpful. He influenced all of us, until each of us worked our way into our own pattern and style. I read many writers of horror and fantasy: Ambrose Bierce, Oliver Onions. Arthur Machen and M.R. James. I read *Dracula* when I was in the Army, and that was a big influence on me. I read omnivorously. I just gulped down everything. And the reason I later wrote westerns was probably because—even though I always liked western movies—when I was in the hospital in England during World War II, I read two western novels a day for about three months.

RICHARD MATHESON

It isn't so much looking at the dark side of human nature, but looking at the *unusual* side. I have very little patience for mainstream novels that deal with "reality" as it is. I have always enjoyed the books and movies that were about something special; that were out of the ordinary. When I read *Dracula* in my teens—that bowled me over. *King Kong* was one of my favorite movies when I was a kid. I was pretty young when it was made, but I saw a revival of it when I was about twelve. That was much more exciting for me than *Andy Hardy Grows Up* . . . ! And I was very aware when I was writing *The Stepford Wives* of the similarities to *Invasion of the Body Snatchers*, the women changing, one by one. . . .

IRA LEVIN

For me it was sort of a double-barreled inspiration. There were certain books which I enjoyed tremendously. I had such a wonderful experience reading them, that I wanted to create that experience for someone else. Some of the ones that I can remember from when I was a kid were Arthur Conan Doyle's *The Lost World*, some of his Sherlock Holmes stories. Bram Stoker's *Dracula*. I also got off on Stevenson and Lovecraft. Harper Lee's *To Kill A Mockingbird* was another major early influence on me. So books inspired me to want to write books. The other thing that influenced me to write was that, as I got older, I read certain books and said to myself: "I can write as good a book as this!" This inspired me to write as much as the great books I'd read in my youth. It wasn't that they were bad books, it was just that there was something in those books that I could identify with, that allowed me to realize, "I can do this—I can really do this." So there were books that made me want to write, and there were books that made me think I could write.

JOSEPH A. CITRO

I was *always* interested in horror. But I think the story that really made me want to write it was "The October Game" by Ray Bradbury. To use the old cliché, that just "blew my mind." It literally left me with my mouth hanging open when I was done. I was 13 at the time I read it, and I did not see that ending coming: "Then . . . some idiot turned on the lights."

Yet that's the way it ends, and you have to go and take the next step . . . by yourself. And create that [last] scene in your head. Which I did, and it just blew me away! I said to myself, "My God, I want to do this to someone else."

F. PAUL WILSON

CHAPTER TWO

Working In the Dark

[Writing's] a very healthy way to get rid of people who are inconvenient. On days when people disappoint me, I do a *lot* of writing. In order to survive that day. I get hurt as much as anyone. I mean, the only difference between a writer and anyone else is his ability to survive a little better with the very things that hurt people horribly! So we have the gift of tears—or the gift of laughter. Either one of them. When people hurt us terribly, we either laugh at them—and laugh them out of existence—or we cry them out of existence.

And then learn to laugh again.

RAY BRADBURY

Back in 1974 or 1975, I coined the term "cross-genre," and no one could figure what I was talking about, but now the term is getting wider usage. In my case this means the melding of elements of mystery, suspense, science fiction, horror, adventure—even the love story. But most important to me is telling the tale from *a mainstream point of view*, with mainstream sensitivity.

DEAN KOONTZ

This is where the craft of storytelling comes into play. Whether you're telling a joke or you're writing a horror story, it's still a matter of seducing your listener or your reader.

Someone who puts out the challenge, "Go ahead—scare me!" What do you do? The storyteller must lull that person into such a suspension of disbelief, into such a state of fascination, if you will, that

13

they *forget they even issued the challenge.* That's how you pull the rug out from under them! In many ways it goes back to the dynamics of a joke: you're telling a story in order to create a specific reaction. If it's a joke, you're looking for a laugh. If it's a horror tale—be it in short story, novel, comics, whatever—you're building your little house of straw in order to elicit a sense of fear, a sense of unease.

STEPHEN R. BISSETTE

My most productive hours are from about two to six in the afternoon. I tend to spend my mornings thinking about what I'm going to do, and shaping it in my mind. I discovered that if I tried to put in eight hours, I got four hours of good writing and four hours of . . . rewritable . . . stuff. I generally put it aside for the evening and try not to think about it until the next morning. Though when I'm in the middle of a book, it's hard to; I find then that I'm living in the town that it's set in, not Seattle.

I try to do the whole book in one fell swoop, as it were. I try to do a chapter a day. And I'll work weekends. Generally speaking, when I'm in the throes of that first draft, it's written start to finish with no breaks.

JOHN SAUL

I loved the conventions! It wasn't a matter of being faithful to them, I loved them! That was the whole idea, to take the clichés: the man in the cloak, the pale face, the flickering gaslights, the struggling victims. To take all the clichés and weave them into something completely different. That's really the key to all my work: to take those clichés and conventions—which I call classic—and then attempt to find a new depth.

ANNE RICE

People are always asking that question: "How long does it take to write a book?" You just look at them and say, "I don't know!" Some books are very quick, though. *The Manitou* was written very quickly— in about two weeks. I don't know if having a word processor now has speeded things up; I don't use as much correcting fluid . . . ! The word processor *has* made my desk tidier, though. I'm usually quite fast as a writer, in any case. But it depends. You can labor all day over a single paragraph, and sometimes you can't write anything at all. I've never really suffered from writer's block, but one is confidently trying to drag the very best out all the time.

GRAHAM MASTERTON

You are supposed to burrow under the reader's skin. And unsettle them. [Stephen King] sometimes uses the word "hurt," which is a wonderful word, in a way, because it sounds so violent! Sometimes you want to "hurt" these readers. But at the same time you don't want to hurt them too badly—I mean, you *do* want to hurt them very badly at a couple points—but you don't want to leave them that way.
PETER STRAUB

I will never live long enough to write all that I want to write. That's the truth. I've never had a writer's block; I never worry about running out of ideas.
CHARLES L. GRANT

I use a word processor. I start work usually at eight-thirty in the morning and work until six, with a half hour off for lunch. I work five, maybe six days a week, maybe seven days a week depending how intensive a schedule it is. While I'm writing one book, there's usually two or three other ideas I'm working on in the back of my mind. It takes me anywhere from a year to ten years for a book to gestate, about nine months to a year to write it. By the time I'm writing it, the book's usually been written and rewritten ten times in my head! And then I usually go between three and ten drafts of a book.
WHITLEY STRIEBER

What really interests me is the way human beings create their own environments, and also the way they rationalize themselves into a situation that's obviously totally insane and yet it somehow still seems rational. To see humans trying to figure out who they are and why they are is what fascinates me.
DAVID CRONENBERG

I came to be interested in jazz while I was writing *Dreamthorp*. There's a character in there who's a serial killer and his father is a professional jazz musician. And in order to make this character sound believable, I went out and bought some jazz records. I bought the Smithsonian collection of classic jazz, which is a nice overview, and I just fell in love with this stuff. I just went crazy over it! So now, some two years later, I have a jazz collection of over 800 albums, I have a small library of books on the subject, and I'm playing the tenor saxophone.
CHET WILLIAMSON

But because [*Off Season*] was so extreme—I felt it was so extreme, and I wanted it, purposely, to be so extreme—I was a little worried about how my family would take it. My father, mother, aunts, uncles, whomever. So I decided, "I'll stick with the pseudonym for this one." I had worked under other pseudonyms before for various men's magazines, so I wasn't uncomfortable with the idea. As it turned out, my whole family was thrilled and delighted that I had even published a book, and weren't worried too much about the content at all.

Then I thought, "There's probably somebody out there looking for another Jack Ketchum book, why change my name now?" So I've just kept it ever since.

JACK KETCHUM

I'm always trying very hard to find a new hole to pop out of. New areas to work in. The novels that I've written have been as different from each other as is possible within the realms of the *fantastique*. The novel that I'm working on now will again be a major departure; there are certainly large areas of fictional life that I want to investigate. That I haven't even begun to touch upon. What I *don't* want to do is repeat myself. I finished up on the *Books of Blood* feeling that I had discharged my duty to short horror fiction as best I could. I don't want to go back over old ground. I owe that to my audience, I owe that to myself, to my craft. My craft is my major way of explaining myself *to* myself.

I don't want to be repeating old adventures. I want to be finding new adventures. I hope that I do have an audience now that will follow me from one genre to another. I hope I'm not given a freedom in the negative sense of just being able to run around, doing whatever I like. But rather be given a latitude to investigate new ideas and know that the audience is going to say, "Well, Clive Barker's got his name on it—we'll give it a go." It allows me a sense of . . . addressing the adventure properly.

CLIVE BARKER

Generally I try to be as awful as I can be. At certain times I want there to be real *shocks*, because in a way that's part of the appeal. And this is something I learned from Steve [King]: that there's no point in exercising too much restraint in this field, because it's enormous fun to be scared in a big, gaudy, splashy way.

PETER STRAUB

I don't cry when they die, but I do get totally wrapped up in the characters, the plot, the whole thing. It's a very draining experience, yet I do have control over it. It takes a *lot* to frighten myself nowadays. When there's a scary moment—yes, I'm very, very tense. I find I'm more scared if I relate that scary moment in that book when I'm talking to people.

For instance if I was in a pub, and was asked "What did you write today?," I would actually go through this scene of horror. *That's* when I would find the hair on the back of my neck standing up—when I'm doing it verbally. *That's* when I get that chill. When I'm writing it, I get a certain kind of chill, but I'm in control. But when I'm describing it, it's like I've reverted back to Jim Herbert—not James Herbert the writer—and it's almost like me telling a scene from a movie I've just seen, or from a story I've just read. The audience part of me comes to the fore, not the author part.

JAMES HERBERT

Resignation, not satisfaction, sets in around deadline time.

THOMAS TESSIER

In *Midnight's Lair*, *One Rainy Night*, *Island*, and a few others, I've basically taken a scary situation and stuck with it until the very end [in "real time"], and made an entire novel out of it. I like to do that once in awhile, because it's fun to start out at a sprint, and then try and keep going at that pace throughout the entire book. It's a real interesting challenge; but you have to pick the right subject matter to make it work.

. . . Most of my novels generally occur within a matter of hours or a couple of days. It gives them a sort of natural unity.

When I'm watching a movie on TV with my family, some of these movies just don't go anywhere. It's become a kind of joke in my family, because I would always comment, "You know what this film doesn't have? It's got no Forward Narrative Thrust." Now I don't even have to say it; I just look at my daughter and she says, "No Forward Narrative Thrust." But—you can pack a *lot* of forward narrative thrust into something that takes place within a very restricted amount of time. You don't need to deal with things which aren't really relevant—you just plow forward.

RICHARD LAYMON

When I was writing [my second collection] *Demons By Daylight*, I really did have an enormous sort of vulnerable sense that I was doing something that nobody else has done before. Whether this is true I'm not at all certain, but I certainly thought I was going out on a limb, that "God, nobody's going to like this!" Because I was picking up fiction by others and saying to myself, "This isn't how you do it—but maybe I'm getting it wrong because these guys are doing it a different way." When I completed the book and packaged it up for August Derleth, I actually thought that he wasn't going to like it, that he was going to send the manuscript straight back, that it was terrible, that he wasn't going to want to touch it! So to have people say, "We think that you got it right," is just what I needed, basically. What can I say? It appears I must be doing something right.

RAMSEY CAMPBELL

One of the things that has comforted me about my own work is that, in almost all cases, I've begun with a premise that was really *black*. And a more pleasant resolution has forced itself upon that structure. Like in *'Salem's Lot*. I was convinced that everybody was going to die! That's what I wanted to happen in that book. But when it didn't, I didn't try to monkey with that fact because I knew in the end that it was *right* that they not all die.

STEPHEN KING

The first thing I ever considered mailing out was *Interview with the Vampire*, and it was accepted within nine months. It went out because I had a deep, instinctive sense that I had pulled a lot of distinctive elements together for the first time, that the book meant more than I was even aware of, that it had a unity that my earlier work hadn't had. And there had been a depth, an intensity, that had been lacking in my other work.

ANNE RICE

I don't consider myself a "horror writer." I write whatever comes into my head. Some stories are westerns no matter what you do with them; and some are crime stories; and some are horror.

I wrote a story recently that I liked a lot and when I started it, I thought it was going to be a western—as it was. But a western of sorts. Because then a horror element came into it, and the horror element deepened the character of the woman I was writing about. If the horror element hadn't suggested itself, the story would have been all right but nothing special. But the horror element, in relation to this older woman who could not have children, gave the piece much more depth. Most people who have read it think it's one of my better efforts, and I think it is, too. But again, I didn't sit down to write a "horror" story. But I'd been re-reading Bradbury's brilliant *The October Country* and filling my head with all those thoughts and images . . . and they clearly affected my story.

ED GORMAN

I try to write books that deliberately encourage involvement, that have atmosphere, and smells, and strong believability. I always aim to write a book that you're not conscious of having read as a book. Because the greatest compliment I've ever been paid by my readers is when they write or call up to say, "*What happened next?!*" What really happened next was that I shut off the word processor and went to bed. But if that world I created for them existed long enough so that they believed something *did* happen then, then I've gone a long way towards that ultimate Graham Masterton novel that I hope someday to be able to write.

GRAHAM MASTERTON

I sold my first book the summer I was out of high school. It was published under a pen-name about a year later. I had three novels published in 1956. I was involved in playwriting in New York for a time, and I've done a hell of a lot of screenwriting. But I try to produce at least a novel a year. One, I still like to write. Two, I try each time I sit down to write something to make it especially challenging—something I've never done before. When writing becomes boring or difficult or unnecessary to do anymore I'll stop, but I don't foresee that happening. I enjoy working on something—a poem, story, novel, screenplay—every day. Maybe in a way I'm obsessed. That's probably part of it. Maybe in five years I'll retire and take up painting again! If I get the chance to make a movie again, I will. But writing is the main thing I do, and everything else is just a break or change of pace that's refreshing.

JOHN FARRIS

I do [write in longhand]. Because years ago I used to be an art director in advertising. And art was my favorite subject as a kid—I

loved drawing and painting. So for me, nowadays, writing is like drawing pictures on the page.
JAMES HERBERT

I write more or less instinctively—I try to write books that I would read if I hadn't written them.
LES DANIELS

I generally just think, "This is the story I'm telling now. I will tell it to the best of my ability." I don't worry if I'm "topping" the last story or not. I don't worry if my audience is going to accept it or not. I don't think about my audience, and that's not an insult to the readers. I certainly care about the readers. But when I sit down behind the typewriter, *fuck the readers!* What I'm interested in then is *me* as a writer, or otherwise I cannot get this story down. And if I start worrying about my readership, then I'm going to repeat myself and burn out either me or my readers. Or I'm going to bore myself, which in that case, why not dig a ditch?
JOE R. LANSDALE

Horror, of course, is pure plot. Some people write "ooze horror," but I write "incident horror." It's one thing after another in a startling fashion but without being so gross that the reader shuts the book.
DAVID MORRELL

I never "just" edit an anthology, or "just" write a novel, or "just" create short fiction. I find it wonderfully healthy to be able to go to various parts of your mind and probe. And that's what I'm doing. I've written at every hour of the day of the twenty-four, and I've begun projects as late as three or four o'clock in the morning. Sometimes successfully; other times I've looked at the material and said, "What the hell is *this*?" But there are so many subjects to explore—UFOs and astrology; philosophy and psychology; sports; cosmology and sociology; music—it's endlessly absorbing, and I want to write about *all* of it!
J.N. WILLIAMSON

Each day is a new adventure. I sit there and just let it pour out. If I'm lucky, it pours out!
JAMES HERBERT

The first story I ever wrote was something about a witch. It was in the sixth grade, I think, and the teacher read it out loud to the class. I ended it with a witch's cackle. I think the story I did after that was about werewolves. So my heart was always in there.

RICHARD LAYMON

Everything is hand-written. Always has been and, I suspect, always will be. I don't own a typewriter or a word processor.

It frees me from not thinking in the technical sense of writing. I don't think about putting in a new piece of paper or a new ribbon; I don't think about the machine's hum or any technical process at all. I enter the "dreamscape" I propose, and describe it. When I'm doing my best work, it has the feeling of journalism. In my mind's eye, I'm seeing something very clearly, very strongly, and I'm simply communicating what I'm seeing in the most direct manner possible.

That describes the first draft. The second draft then becomes much more about the way the material is shaped on the page. It becomes a question of refining vocabulary, of refining syntax, and so on. So the hand is there, working away in this very simple manner, in the very first way we learn to put words down: a pen and a piece of paper. I started writing when I was four, and it's certainly served me well . . . so I see no specific reason to change it now.

CLIVE BARKER

When I was still teaching, it used to be that when a student came into my office and said "I want to be a writer," I'd reply, "What defect in your personality accounts for that ambition?" It seems that many of us are writing, inadvertently, because of some inner turmoil that we're trying to get rid of. In my own case, one can find certain themes that reappear with remarkable regularity. There is, for example, the theme of a child and the parent, usually involving a father and a son, but not exclusively.

My biological father died about the time I was born, during World War II. So I grew up during those formative years alone with my mother. Apparently that was very traumatic for me, to find that other children had two parents, and I did not. I was utterly baffled by this, and I'm still trying to work out that bafflement in some of my stories.

It isn't good to think too much about such traumas, because if you were ever to come to terms with whatever it was that's bothering you, then you wouldn't have anything to write about anymore. God knows, I don't want *that* to happen.

DAVID MORRELL

My first horror novel had a real downbeat ending, and a lot of people were upset by that. But I think an ending where things don't turn out rosy is pretty appropriate to a horror story. I'm not obsessed with downbeat endings, but I do have a real appreciation for endings that deal with a sort of poetic justice.

RICHARD LAYMON

A "typical work day" is mostly conducted at night. I live on an odd schedule, which I guess other horror writers have done—Sheridan LeFanu and Lovecraft—but I'm not really doing it to imitate them or be affected. I usually spend the day doing research, going to the library, and reading. By midnight, except on occasions when something colorful comes up, there usually isn't much for me to do, and there's fewer distractions, so that's a good time for me to get started. I sometimes go on even to dawn. It helps for me to know that I have a project, and that somebody is waiting for me to finish it. I'm not one of those writers who has twenty books in a drawer that I wrote for the fun of it, hoping that someday maybe somebody would want them.

LES DANIELS

I'm a late riser. I'm one of those people that for me to go to sleep, it's like another day's work. I dream very heavily, in full technicolour. But I get into the study at ten, and I work through to lunch time, at one o'clock. I'll have lunch, read the morning newspaper, and get back to the study about half past two, and then I'll work through to six o'clock in the evening, and if it's going well, until seven. But that's my deadline; I never work beyond that. Sometimes it's seven days a week, but generally it's six days a week.

JAMES HERBERT

It's not easy to evoke a scare in somebody. It's not easy to take tried-and-true material and make it fresh. You're working in a form that is just about as rigid as the Western story, and they aren't publishing Westerns any more for a lot of reasons. And one of them is that the public got bored because there wasn't anything more to say.

This may happen to horror fiction, though I think the latitude is wider.

But working up to a good scare scene is difficult to do, and that's the heart of it. At this point, it's simply a case of talent coming into play; some people can do it, some people can't. It's like the difference between Julius Irving on a basketball court and some kid in high school. Dr. J has the moves, and the kid doesn't have them. He can try to emulate them, he can do a pretty good job of dribbling. But going one on one with Dr. J, he's going to get killed! And there are very few writers who have got the moves . . .

JOHN FARRIS

I don't plan.
I don't analyze.
I write intuitively.

THOMAS TESSIER

There's a scene in *Shadowland* [by Peter Straub]—it's my favorite single moment—where this guy looks up from an examination and there's this pencil floating in the air, and Delmar Nightingale sees it and snatches it away because he doesn't want anyone else to see it. But that's the essence of the attraction the supernatural story has for me: *that pencil just floating there in the air*. It's like those Magritte paintings where trains are coming out of fireplaces, Dali paintings where clocks are lying over branches.

In "The Mist," for instance, the great attraction in a story like that to me was I really I don't *care* what causes it, or anything else. It's the idea of that train coming out of the fireplace. The familiar juxtaposed with the unusual and the strange. That, to me, is the attraction.

STEPHEN KING

I think I'm slightly moving away from the ancient demon type of book . . . but there were so many interesting and unusual terrors of the past. One reason I wanted to go back and look at them is because some time in the past they really *did* terrify some cultures. It's quite interesting to explore what it was about them that made them so frightening. Exploring certain fears like being visited by the dead; that comes up as zombies and ghouls. Fears of being dragged under by strange maidens, fears of being made love to in the night by disgusting creatures . . . !

I also like to have something of an intellectual game with the reader, with those who have a long standing interest in horror stories, and have knowledge of their background. By getting in little jokes and word-plays which refer back to old H.P. Lovecraft stories or other stories they may have read. It's kind of a "short-hand of horror" in that you *know* it's going to be frightening once you start mentioning Arkham or going the wrong way by the Miskatonic River. You just add layers to the horror. And to those who know these mythologies, it's an added pleasure.

GRAHAM MASTERTON

For me, [*Queen of the Damned*] was the first book in which I really used the computer as the pure poetic tool it is capable of being. Because what the computer enables you to do is range back and forth across your work, and bring it up to your standards very easily.

So even my smallest dissatisfactions, things I might have put up with if it had been typewritten, I was quickly able to boot up on the computer and change. So that's what I mean by pure and poetic: the computer really enables you to get *exactly* what you want to get. There's really no physical barrier anymore between you and your vision. If you can get it into words, you can really create what you see.

On the typewriter, I don't think that's true. You reach a point where you have this big, ponderous draft, and even to make minor changes in early chapters would mean making a mess, losing control of pages, having to retype. You're dealing with the industrial revolution; you're dealing with a mechanism, with labor . . . and all of that's swept away by the computer; there's very little between your mind and what you're putting down there. There's really no excuse for not writing the perfect book. You're no longer making the mechanical compromises that move it away from poetry. I see poetry as meaning language at its very finest, and its most intense and most compressed. And you're able to get that essence with a computer.

ANNE RICE

I really enjoy small towns. Because in a small town everybody knows everybody, and everybody's involved in everyone else's business. When something goes haywire, everybody immediately knows about it—and is immediately terrified about it. Whereas the same thing could happen in a major city, and 99% of the population would never even know it was happening. It's much easier to build a great level of suspense in a small town. Also, the smaller and more isolated the town, the easier it is to have no one around to quickly figure out what's happening, or to put a stop to it. As for children, usually in my books the villain is also the prime victim. And that works best with children, as there is an assumption that children are not necessarily responsible for their actions. If you have somebody who's an adult doing what my kids are doing, there's no sympathy for them.

JOHN SAUL

My work is a great joy. I wouldn't be able to tell you exactly what it is that drives me, but I have *lots* of ideas. I have hundreds of ideas, and they're just stacked up in a holding pattern. I've got ten novel ideas that I really would like to do, and I can't get to them all! I write like a madman, I write as fast as I can, and I still can't get to them all. By the time I'm finished with one thing, I have five additional ideas, and then I'll have two *more* ideas, for a total of seven ideas . . . !

WHITLEY STRIEBER

[If I wasn't writing about the dark side of human nature] I would probably be a comedy writer.

There's a humorous side to the horrible, too. But horror is difficult to do, and so is humor. Few writers do well in either genre. I'm not an expert on other people's horror, because frankly I don't read a lot of it. I can't speak for other horror writers, and I don't know if I'm morbid by nature. I don't think so. I am deeply cynical. I'm always appalled by human nature yet fascinated by the contradictions, the perversity of people. Most of us are perverse. You just need to sit back and be tolerant or amused by it all.

JOHN FARRIS

Humor and horror both invoke a reaction by means of shock and/or surprise. Both make effective use of the same element—the unexpected. I use either in order to the startle the reader; I find this help keeps him awake.

ROBERT BLOCH

When I'm doing something that's funny and I don't laugh, it's not going to make anybody else laugh. As far as being scary is concerned, if it doesn't scare me, it's not going to scare anybody else. If I say to myself, "Oh, that's *too* strong, I shouldn't use that!" then I say, 'Wait a minute—use it!' Because then I know I'm on to something here, and I don't throw it away.

If I don't get a *frisson*, then you won't get a *frisson*. And of course there's no such thing as a *free-son*.

GAHAN WILSON

There's a piece of me in all my characters. It's like the old line, "We are multitudes." I've always felt we hold many, many people within us, and many, many emotions. And that when you write, you just peel off layers until you reach certain people. Sometimes that can get kind of fun and scary and very dark. I think there is a potential in all of us for doing evil, horrible things. But because of our upbringing, society, and nice little things like that, we are able to cover those over. But they still exist way deep down inside us, and we as writers can delve down into those places. I think that's why I named my villain in *McKain's Dilemma* Carlton Runnells, because Carlton is my middle name. So there are all sorts of people inside all of us, and they pop out now and again.

CHET WILLIAMSON

If a novel of mine was to have the ultimate effect on the reader, it would be a novel in which the reader would be reading the story, and look up, and find out he is reading it *for real*. Then they would have to put the book down and deal—*for real*—with the terror to which they've been introduced. If they can survive long enough to finish the book, that's the only way they'll do it. How I would love to do that!

GRAHAM MASTERTON

I don't work that hard. I write every day, but I limit that to two or three hours. Sometimes I'll write my two or three hours late at night— I'll slip out of bed, go downstairs, and write from about two in the morning, and go to bed about four. But I don't let the writing interfere with my leisure time, with my personal life. I'm fortunate in that I can turn it on any time of the day or night and the material flows. If I don't write one day, then I don't feel quite as good. I don't feel terrible, but I just don't feel quite as happy.

LARRY COHEN

I find that almost all the books which have been coming out for the last few years are written with a very deliberate hero and/or heroine in mind. People I usually think of as "Betty and Bob," who are the wonderful folks who live in the suburbs, and are a cute couple, and have a kid. And something BAD is going to happen to them! And the book is usually about how Betty and Bob managed to overcome "it." Sometimes only Betty manages to overcome "it." Sometimes only Bob. . . . But I find that much less interesting to me—I want to get in and deal with the parts that are frightening. Having these sort of TV-style "nice folks" taking up the bulk of the book, and for me to be expected to really worry about them . . . !

LES DANIELS

I live in the Hollywood Hills overlooking Los Angeles, and I have this job-robbing view. When I go out and look at this view, I can't write a word. You just become mesmerized. I have to go downstairs, to what looks like a closet, and be very uncomfortable. I have my typewriter facing a wall, with a light over my shoulder, and a calendar which shows when my deadline is. It's like cramming for a final, because writing is not fun. Stephen King must love it—he must love to play with words. I *hate* playing with words. I'd much rather direct: "Let's get a scene here! You come in that door, we'll drop the fire on you, and we'll do this next!" No, I have a totally different approach to writing. I have to get into such a state, mentally, because it really takes such an enormous amount of commitment and dedication. You just can't indulge yourself when you write. And I really am lazy. And I really enjoy being lazy. So that's my confession about writing.

JOHN CARPENTER

It's gotten so that there are so many fascinating things that one can do. And the discipline of it alone is so interesting. Because you're dealing with the occult and the supernatural—remember we were just talking about mythologies?—well, there have to be some kind of ground rules. Otherwise, there is no fear. Without ground rules, your hero cannot overcome the demon, or the other way around. So, in some ways, writing horror is *much* more difficult than writing any other kind of book because you have to create your own discipline, your own ground rules, and then have to stick with them.

GRAHAM MASTERTON

You know you're really a writer when you're reading something and you find yourself stopping, going back, finding the paragraph or passage that really affected you in some way. And you say to yourself,

"Wow! What did he do that worked so well?" So you go back, and find that passage. And you put up it on the lift, and you look under the chassis of that paragraph, and you realize then what made it work.

Then you know you're really a writer, because that's what we do that most readers don't.

But then there is that extra special moment, when you get caught up in the experience so totally that you forget about all that, that you forget that this is simply a reading experience, that's what Stephen King did, for example, in *The Shining*. You become so totally trapped in the experience to a point where you physically have to stop and say to yourself, "I can't this read this. I've got to pull myself out." Now *that's* really effective writing! Only much later can you take it apart, and try to figure out how he did it.

THOMAS F. MONTELEONE

The work is never as good at the end as it was when I started. I start the first page and know that this is going to be an absolutely *fabulous* book, and I'm going to do all these wonderful things in it. And when I get to the end, I always find that I really haven't been able to pull it off, everything that I had originally wanted to do. So I'm never as happy at the end [of a project] as I am at the beginning.

With a short story I can usually say, "Yes, I've accomplished what I wanted." But it's been accomplished on a much narrower scope. I would say *Sibs* is the closet I came to being completely satisfied on a novel, because I wrote it in something like nine weeks. I was actually exhausted at the end. I felt like I wasn't writing, I was taking dictation. So when I look back on it, I can say, "God, if I could do that with every book, what a career I would have!"

But usually it's just: "Well, it's not what I wanted, but it's the best I can do at this time." And hopefully, I've learning something from this book, and with the next one I'll get a little closer to what I'm after.

F. PAUL WILSON

The reason Stephen King said "The author who influenced me most as a writer was Richard Matheson" . . . was because as a young man he was reading H.P. Lovecraft, and early Bob Bloch, and a lot of it was real Gothic—graveyards, castles, crypts. And I started writing novels in the Fifties that took place in suburban neighborhoods. *I Am Legend*, for God's sake, takes place in Gardena, California. And Robert Neville finds bodies in the back of supermarkets, rather than crypts.

That apparently opened up a world of possibilities for King. And many other writers, I guess. I wrote one novelette in that [Gothic] style just to see if I could do it. But that's not the way I think—I'm a realist. Whatever success I've had is because I am a realist: I make whatever I write about seem very realistic. I can only set my stories in realistic settings that I readily understand. I can't do haunted castles and dungeons. Or mystic kingdoms with little trolls running around . . . I admire people who can do that—one of my favorite books is *The Sword In The Stone*. And I admire J.R.R. Tolkein a great deal. But I can't write that kind of fantasy.

RICHARD MATHESON

The assumption I always have when I'm writing is this happened. This is real. I have to describe it to the reader, but it's not something I'm making up. It really happened.

IRA LEVIN

It's something I've always felt as a storyteller—to keep you in suspense. Mainly, to keep your interest! I've never thought of it as writing in a "suspenseful way." It's just that I need to keep you in suspense in order to take you down this road. In any movie that I've ever written, I've always felt that I had an element of suspense, because I think that's my style of telling a story. I always make clear-cut decisions about when I'm going to tell you something I want you to know—or when I'm not going to tell the audience—or when to let you in on something the character hasn't been let in on. This is the way I've always gone—to keep you interested as long as possible with suspense and then in a way reward you at the end for having remained interested.

JOSEPH STEFANO

CHAPTER THREE

Short Story, Novel, or Script?

I wrote both [forms] when I was just starting out, though I had short stories published before I sold my first novel. I think there are several aspects to this situation. One is that a lot of people in the horror field—and the mystery field too—spend a *lot* of time concentrating just on short stories. That is, they focus all their time and attention on short stories, and postpone coming out with a novel. I think that's a mistake, because it's only with a novel that you're actually going to focus some attention on yourself as a writer. And it's also where you're going to have any chance of making some money. If you want to have a career as a writer, you *have* to write novels—not just short stories.

By the same token—perhaps the opposite one!—writing short stories is a great way to learn how to write fiction. You just can't fake it within a short story—not if you have a good editor, you can't! But by writing short stories you can actually learn just what a "story" is. This is not something I think you can teach anyone, but it *is* something you can develop a sense of by the practice of writing short stories. Short stories are also a way of breaking into the field, and getting your name out for the first time. So I recommend writing them, but not sticking with 'em too long. Write them long enough to put them on your resume, and to help someone—like an agent!—to pay attention to your novel.

RICHARD LAYMON

I can't look at one of my books and try and make it into a screenplay. Why? Because I'll look at something and I know why it was there in the novel, and I'll think it also has to be there in the

screenplay. Adapting a novel to the screen is not the shortcut many people like to think it is. In many cases it can be a longer and more tortuous process because you keep thinking of what you have to put in.
MICHAEL McDOWELL

It's certainly easier writing novels now than it was when I first started; I'd rather write a novel than a short story these days. Now I don't tend to have a preconceived plot, whereas before, even with a short story, I would have a pretty clear idea of its structure and point of view. But I was a bit afraid of finding myself halfway through a novel and discovering I didn't know where the hell I was going next! Of course, that does happen, but I now find it interesting simply to find out where the novel is going. I mean, novels actually *do* go on their own momentum, and really build their own structures. I think if you can take that risk of not conceiving everything in advance, the novel actually becomes very organic, and I find that very satisfying.
RAMSEY CAMPBELL

Writing short stories is infinitely harder than writing a novel. But you get ideas that just won't support a novel, and besides, I *like* to write short stories. They're fun. And they make you practice your craft with a lot more diligence than a novel does. In a novel you're tempted to run around a lot, but in a short story every word has to count. So it's good practice. And practically speaking, it help keeps your name out before the public when there aren't any of your books out.
CHARLES L. GRANT

As a creator, I get more of a buzz from comics than I do from anything else. I cannot go back and look at a short story or a novel that's come out with pleasure. Rather I look at it and think, "Oh God, I should have fixed that." Whereas I can look at a comic I've done and get a real buzz off it and have a real feeling of pride. It's always a feeling of surprise to me when something that I wrote as a script comes out and it actually *works*. And it's a very pleasant surprise because I didn't really "do" it—all I ever did was *write* it. Knowing that the script for a comic is *not* the comic. The comic is the comic.
NEIL GAIMAN

I find that what happens to me—particularly as I get older—is that I just don't have the energy to devote the whole block of time, the whole three or four months scheduled, completely to it. I often thought about writing a novel, but then I realize what a commitment that is. Screenplays are in fact about one third the size. On the other hand, they do need more careful outlining, because they are much more concise. They're not as forgiving in terms of letting you roam. So I find that it's a process that's sort of like doing a jigsaw puzzle. It requires a certain period of really concentrated thought, which has more to do with organizing and trying to figure out what's really important. Every writer goes through that. Then the actual physical writing—particularly dialogue—what I do is usually leave all the dialogue until the end and try not to think about it; to try to not constipate the dialogue. I find that if I get preconceived speeches in my head, then I start refining them and pretty soon they sound like people.

So I let that go as sort of that final coat, which is that three or four week period when I actually put it into the proper format in the word processor. That's working from notes and whatever else, little thoughts and ideas. I have a portable tape recorder in my car. And I'll just jot things. This has probably evolved through convenience, because I just want more time with my family. I find that when I am in the final stage of writing I very often have to actually move out of the house. We have two houses, so I'm lucky that way. But if we're all in Florida, I'll just go and rent a joint on the beach and sit there and eat Spam until I'm finished.

GEORGE A. ROMERO

I adapted Henry Kuttner's "The Graveyard Rats," [and two other stories to] form a Movie of the Week called *Trilogy of Terror II*. Actually, the Kuttner segment is practically an original. All I started with—in the published story—was a character who gets trapped underground in a graveyard and has to battle a horde of killer rats. That's all I had to work with. I had no conflict, no developing dramatic situation, no build-up, no interesting characters. I had to create 90% of that story. The last three pages—the last three minutes on the television screen—will be Henry Kuttner's "The Graveyard Rats." So, again, we have a collaboration—in terms of adapting another writer's short story.

WILLIAM F. NOLAN

Interview with the Vampire was a short story first, but I just didn't pursue short stories; they don't interest me now. The long form is what interests me. And frankly, I think you should go where the passion is. Many, many people start with novels. There is also a very practical concern: it's easier to sell a novel than it is a short story. There's almost no market for short stories in America; they don't reach the public or have the impact that a novel makes. And in terms of career, anyone who writes novels is going to have it easier than a short story writer.

But that shouldn't be the main concern either. The main concern is that you should do what you feel comfortable doing. I feel comfortable stretching it out. Going at it from all angles. I don't want to compress it into a short story. I really don't. Almost any idea that really grips me is worth a novel.

ANNE RICE

One of my problems—if you can call it a problem—is I run away from the herd. If everybody else is doing it, I don't want to do it. The only short stories I've done—one of them was for charity, and that's been used in various anthologies and publications until everybody's probably sick of it. And that was taken from a novel that New American Library, who used to publish me, they knocked it out. And rather than waste it, I offered it up as a short story. It was called "Breakfast" and was about the final holocaust. The other reason is I don't have time. I really don't have time to sit down and write a short story when I'm too heavily involved in doing "full-length" stories.

JAMES HERBERT

First, I like to believe my novels are thrillers with a difference. If you ripped off the title page, and put my novels side by side with a group of other writers' thrillers—so you couldn't know who composed what—you'd see that most thriller writers look as if they've been reading each other, and are all doing essentially the same kind of book. But with me, I think what you'd find would be a distinctive mix of the eerie, the insane, the horrific, lurking alongside the action in the story, and at a certain point, the combination explodes upon the reader. Hopefully, with appropriately satisfying results. Now, with the short story—and I pretty much decided that my short work would be in the horror field—there is nothing lurking; I have the horrific situation in mind, and I always try to keep that horror at the center of the effect that I'm trying for. I have found those stories come easiest for me when I write in the first person. I had a block for many years

writing stories, and I happened to be rereading Browning, and came upon what are known as his "dramatic monologues." I just loved the way he was doing these poems, and I suddenly said, "What if I made my short stories the equivalent of dramatic monologues? In which the first person addressed the audience to tell them what was going on?" On the face of it, this doesn't sound like a great revelation, but it was for me. The first person suddenly seemed a new technique.
David Morrell

I usually start out by looking for a novel-length idea, or a short story-length idea. Off-hand, I can't recall them ever crossing paths. I have taken old short stories and put them into novels on a couple of occasions. In *Tread Softly*, the tales told around the campfire had, on a couple of occasions, in fact already been written up earlier as short stories.
Richard Laymon

There is an *endless* amount of untapped potential in the comic medium. And the further I get into it, the bigger it seems. In just doing the first four or five issues of *Big Numbers*, I managed to think of three or four entirely *new* things that have not been done in comics before. And this is just me—this is just *one* person following their own individual ideas. Yes, it gets progressively harder to think of new ways to use the language of comics, but that doesn't diminish in any way the fact that those new ways are still out there. I can easily imagine the younger talents who aren't so hollow and jaded as myself who will be able to unearth some real gems along the way. I think there are possibilities for the comic medium that have yet to be *imagined*. Comics are an ancient language, going back to the Chinese ideograms, and what we're doing here is establishing the most basic grammar and vocabulary. I hope that later generations will be able to use this grammar and vocabulary to compose magnificent works. We've barely scratched the surface of what can be done! I mean, when you've got the whole world of words and pictures in conjunction to play with, then you've got *everything* at your disposal.

There is *nothing* that comics cannot do. There is nothing that has been attempted in any other artistic medium that comics could not, eventually, equal or better. It's up to the people who are alive at this time to explore the language as thoroughly as possible, to find their own themes, and to follow their own individual, quirky paths. And follow them relentlessly.

ALAN MOORE

I had a wanted to be a novelist early on—even before I was out of college. I always wanted to be one, but got kind of side-tracked into the film business. I like the film business too, but growing up I never thought I could be a movie-maker. I was one of those people who thought that only happened to those living and working in Hollywood. But when I started doing short films with George Romero, then that idea became more real. My writing skills improved because of the number of TV commercials I had to do, the industrial films, promotional writing, and what that does is sharpen your skills through sheer experience. After I did the novelization of *Night of the Living Dead,* it became easier for me sell other books because of the success of that film and the book. It may make it harder to sell something else, but you find that working in this genre you find out you can explore just about *any* kind of theme anyway. You can really do just about anything you want to do in this genre.

JOHN RUSSO

I've been working on [Peter Straub's] *Floating Dragon* to make it a two-hour television movie. And it's a real toughie. I had to eliminate a great deal of material from the book, including a major subplot. In a two-hour television film, you don't really have two hours; because of commercials, you have 97 minutes of actual screen time. And since one script page equals a minute of screen time, we're talking about a 97 page script for *Floating Dragon* from a 515 page novel that has all kinds of characters, viewpoints, and subplots. It becomes a matter of selection and compression.

Sometimes you'll take three or four characters from the novel and combine their characteristics into one person. Let's say for example you have a newspaper editor, a reporter, and a photographer that are working together on a story. You might combine all those into the editor of the newspaper, and make it a small newspaper so that he has to do his own photography and his own research. But you'll use parts of the character's dialogues and their actions in the novel for your screenplay. So it is a compression situation. When I had finished my first long outline I had created new material and compressed old material. I sent the treatment to Peter in New York and he told me how much he liked it—then presented me with 47 pages of notes! But actually they were "detail" notes, not "basic approach" notes; he was indeed happy with the way I'd handled his book. I kept his notes in mind in doing the final draft of the treatment.

I tried like hell to adapt [his] *Shadowland*. But I could not lick that book! It's an illusionary novel, and much of it is in the mind of the narrator. I couldn't find a way to visually translate it. The first job of every screenwriter is to say, "Can this be visually transformed into script format? Some books can't be done—by me or anyone else. Books are sometimes bought by producers simply because of the name of the author or because they're bestsellers and the producers want to brag that "we have the movie rights to so-and-so."
WILLIAM F. NOLAN

[For beginning novelists] the tried-and-true method is to outline. But I don't outline, so I'm really being hypocritical here. But that's the way my work methods evolved. I can't outline. But for a new writer, I would suggest they write themselves a ten or fifteen page synopsis. Write it all in the present tense. In that way you've at least got some guidelines to work with. But as I said, I don't—the book's in my head when I'm ready to write. And I don't start writing it until I'm ready to, and then I just write it. Not every blessed little scene—but the basic structure is in my head, so I know what's going to happen.

I see it as a movie up there in my brain, and I just write down what I'm looking at. I don't see it as a narrative flow; I see scenes. Specific scenes. I've got a bunch of scenes in my head now for the new novel; if I can put them into words it'll be really great stuff!
CHARLES L. GRANT

Short stories are a way to learn method, to get a lot of mistakes out of your system without investing months in a novel that you may not have the technical experience to accomplish. You finally see that the novel isn't working, and if you had accumulated some experience writing short stories, you might earlier have sensed a warning signal from your subconscious telling you to stop. John Barth once told me that, when he was starting a novel, he tried various approaches that he called "test borings." And I said, "Oh, I see. It's like drilling to see if there's oil or gold down there." He looked at me for a minute and said, "No, I want to see if the material *bores* me."
DAVID MORRELL

That's why I find comics so interesting. The way that people read comics and the way they read prose is a different experience. I believe a lot of people don't read prose with the amount of attention and effort that they give to comic books. In a comic book they will read *every* picture, and *every* word and be forced by the juxtaposition to look at how these things relate to each other.

People skip when they read prose. People skip words, they skip pages, sometimes they skip thoughts. Or they flip through pages. Or they read it faster and less attentively than they read other sections. A writer has no control over how somebody reads.

In comics, you have a lot more control over the experience of reading. Over what and how the person reading it reads. You are doling out pieces of information to them with an immediacy that they otherwise might not have.

NEIL GAIMAN

With a novel, you have this great mass of material, with subplots and multiple characters, that must be compressed for the screen. A book can bend in all kinds of directions, like a pretzel. But a script has to have a direct dramatic arc which must build, crest, and then pay off in the end.

WILLIAM F. NOLAN

I never discriminated—in the racial sense of the term—between comics and anything else I read. I was a voracious reader as a kid; I read anything and everything. And one of the things I read was comics. I couldn't understand why there was any kind of prejudice against them; why we weren't allowed to bring them to school. Why was it something everyone sort of frowned on? Books were considered cool, and yet there was as much thought and artistry in a lot of the comics that I was reading . . . So I never discriminated; I never felt that comics were in any way a "lesser" medium. They seemed to me a *more* exciting medium: I always figured I would be a writer when I grew up, and one of the things I always wanted to write was comics.

And here I am.

NEIL GAIMAN

Short stories have two functions for a novelist. One is that after I finish a long piece of fiction, I sometimes find I have a little juice, a little creative energy, left over. And I don't want to start into anything major, but while I'm still primed after finishing a book, it seems like the right time to go in and do a short story. I'm therefore able to do something relatively quickly and get something accomplished between major projects. There's a special pleasure in finishing a story within a few weeks, after having labored a year or more to finish a novel.

The other thing is, short stories by definition depict ideas that are usually not of sufficient scope to merit a novelistic treatment, yet the ideas themselves might have a wonderful potential and perfect legitimacy. So I have a number of ideas that occur to me when I'm working on a novel, and when I'm done, I reconsider these ideas. Many no longer seem worth the time it would take to turn them into stories, but some have grown better in my mind and I can't resist the impulse to play with them.

DAVID MORRELL

This is really a *major* difference between writing prose fiction and writing comics. There is something so solitary in writing prose fiction: you're creating a world entirely out of your own material. It's as rewarding in some ways, but it's . . . different. The aspect that I most enjoy working in comics is the meeting of minds and the meeting of sensibilities. It's like some kind of cultural sex for me; to grasp what someone else is feeling is thrilling in an intellectual and creative way. This cross-fertilization between different imaginations! And the key to making that work, in my own experience, is the empathy the writer has with the artist, of thinking in pictures that *they* might have created.

ALAN MOORE

Let's face it, film and television writing is a collaborative medium all down the line. There are usually more than a hundred people involved in each production. You end up "collaborating" with the set designer, the art director, the wardrobe and makeup people, the special effects experts, the unit production manager—and each actor, as well. Not to mention the considerable input a writer usually receives from network or studio executives. So you go into it with that sort of mind-set. Every person has his or her own particular vision of what the finished product should be, so you can see that collaboration is the very basis of television and film production. In the initial stage of collaborative writing you try to work with people who operate on your creative wave length; you look for a creative rapport.

With prose work, it's just you and the page—and the only "collaborator" you've got is your editor. With scripting, it's like working on a circus. All kinds of people have input into the final product. I always say that if a writer can't tolerate collaboration, he or she should stay away from scripting. Prose writing helps keep me sane. I'd go wacko if I just did scripts without the novels and the stories and articles in between to balance things out.

WILLIAM F. NOLAN

The Axman Cometh began as a story. I thought of the premise the day before I started to write. Originally it was two short stories which came together in my mind as one ... I conceived the story on the fourteenth of August, sat down to write it on the fifteenth, and on the twenty-fourth of October, it was done as a full-length novel. I didn't know when I sat down this would happen! Although I always had a notion of where I meant to go with the idea, I didn't know who most of the characters were until they popped up while I was writing. My expectation was only that I wanted to find out what happened next.

JOHN FARRIS

What it comes down to in comics is that you have complete control of both the verbal track and the image track, which you don't have in any other medium, including film. So a lot of effects are possible which simply cannot be achieved anywhere else. You control the words and the pictures—and more importantly—you control the *interplay* between those two elements in a way which not even film can achieve. There's a sort of "under-language" at work there, that is neither the "visuals" nor the "verbals," but a unique effect caused by a combination of the two.

A picture can be set against text ironically, or it can be used to support the text, or it can be completely disjointed from the text—which forces the reader into looking at the scene in a new way. You can do this to some extent in film, in terms of striking interesting juxtapositions between the imagery and what the intent of the characters may be, but you cannot do it anywhere near as precisely as you can in comics. Here the reader has the ability to stop and linger over one particular "frame" and work out *all* of the meaning in that frame or panel, as opposed to having it flash by you at twenty-four frames per second in a cinema.

ALAN MOORE

Although comics aren't in any way like movies, I have to say that the important role that horror films played in my development as a creative individual plugged me into doing comics. I don't have the means for making movies. Comics are my way of putting down on paper the movies that run in my head. And it allows me to put them down on paper in such a way so you can experience them to the best of my ability and skill.

STEPHEN R. BISSETTE

To me, what's so different about writing a short story is that it's just a little piece of life. And I discover those little pieces mostly through reflection—I seem to find short stories by recalling my own childhood experiences, or things that frightened me while I was growing up. Attempts to deal with the world from the point of view of a six year old kid, or a nine-year-old kid. The world can be pretty monstrous and frightening—and beautiful—from that pre-jaded view of youth. So, in developing my stories, I search for a magical minute, a spark of magic that captures just a little piece of life, and that's what I try to build a short story around. It's the only way I know *how* to write a short story.

JOSEPH A. CITRO

I don't know how this answer will sound, but it's actually true. One form [horror teleplays] has commercials, and the other form [feature screenplays] is much longer. Now, what that means is you have a different rhythm for each. And what's particularly hard is that, not only do you have to think of telling a story, but you've got to have an "electrified story." That is, it's got to produce jolts now and then. A normal screenplay works like one of those little wooden trains that children have that go around a track. But with a horror screenplay, you've got to electrify that track so it produces jolts at certain points along the way.

So, here's what we have. In working for television, for ... thirty minute shows you have a very specific time frame. These are 5-8-8: five minutes, eight minutes, and eight minutes. And you have a progression of jolts in those frames. It's a very tricky business to get everything in there for budgetary considerations, and tell a good story, too. But those are great fun, and they take all of your concentration.

MICHAEL McDOWELL

If you can write a good short story, then you can write anything. The hardest thing to write is a really fine, wonderful, great short story. We can learn from the masters like Poe and Bradbury—and even Lovecraft, even though he had no control of language, he still knew how to tell a damn good short story! But all the elements of good storytelling: of narrative, of character, of plot, of pacing. All the elements that make good writing what it is—what it should be—are demanded of the short story form.

If you can learn how to do that, and learn how to do it well, I truly believe any other narrative form will be a lot easier to solve, technically speaking.

Even if you're tempted to write a novel first, you'll teach yourself a lot more valuable lessons by writing stories, even if you never sell them. You'll learn more about keeping your sentences under control, about pacing, about creating believable characters—a lot of very important elements.

It's not like you're learning shorthand—you're learning how to break the code.

THOMAS F. MONTELEONE

At one time I would have said novels without hesitating. But now I'm not so sure. And it's always difficult to break into the film industry. I was watching Larry King last night and this marvelous Irish step dancer, Michael Flatley, was saying "Follow your dream! Follow your dream!" That's really what it comes down to: *you've got to do what you really love.* You can't work your way into a market simply because it seems like a good market to work your way into.

The last time I looked at the marketplace for short stories, it wasn't that great. You can always get your stories published in "fanzines" and the small press, but in terms of being paid real money for your work, you have maybe *Playboy* and *Omni*—and that's it. Back in the Fifties there were like sixty science fiction magazines—that's why I started writing it. I didn't know anything about science fiction; I had no *idea* what it was. But with sixty magazines out there, I learned pretty fast. I did it because it also gave me the greatest chance of breaking in: I've always been very practical. And at the time, my dreams were kind of muddled. I had no specific area then I wanted most to work in.

RICHARD MATHESON

There are no rules; they should do absolutely what they feel like doing. But I would never advise a person to write short stories if they want to write a novel. There's just no point.

ANNE RICE

CHAPTER FOUR

Regarding Fame and Fortune

Number one: you think you can do it. You think you have the talent to go over the top and earn your living that way. In a way, you feel that's what God meant you to do, you know? You don't feel satisfied with what you're doing because you know that's not what you were meant to do, you know? I won't say I've lead a grim life, but it was—and still is—sort of a humdrum life. It isn't any big deal. I don't go out and ride around in a limousine, sniff cocaine with a babe on each arm. . . . But it's fun—you can go and get away from all that shit. And it's escapism. It's the same reason why people watch TV. But this is like "mind TV" or "mind movies."

The other thing that was always in play with me was I was convinced—*deeply convinced*—that somewhere, deep inside me, was a money machine. Waiting to be turned on. And that when I found the dials and the combinations, the money would just pour out.

It was never a question of I felt I had anything to prove to anyone else. But in a way, with those early [unpublished] novels, I felt like a guy who was plugging quarters in the machine with the big jackpot. And yanking it down. And at first they were coming up all wrong. Then with the book before *Carrie*, I felt I got two bars and a lemon; then with *Carrie* bars across the board—and the money poured out. But the thing is, I was never convinced that I was going to run out of quarters to plug into the machine. My feeling was, I could stand there forever until it hit! There was never really any doubt in my own mind. A couple of times I felt like I was pursuing a fool's dream or something like that, but they were rare.

STEPHEN KING

My first warning would be to stop believing in "destiny." My second warning would be to opt for a less demanding profession. Writing is a lonely occupation, exposing one to constant rejection, criticism and (if one is successful) to jealousy and the malice of the envious. It is, in addition, quite arduous, and it takes its toll in stress. There are also accompanying perils to consider. If you don't watch out, you can end up giving interviews.

ROBERT BLOCH

I've always longed—naturally—for a bigger and bigger readership, and it is getting to be quite a big readership actually, but I always feel that there could have been another half million readers for a particular book. So I'm never satisfied with what I've got. I want more! And it's up to me to get them. I'll get those readers, if I deserve them.

WHITLEY STRIEBER

In defense of the paperback novelist—for the benefit of your readers who want to become writers—the truth of the matter is, that with the exception of a handful of writers at the very top, the average author's hardcover novel will probably have no more than 10 to 12,000 readers if it's minimally successful. The fewest number of readers I ever had for any of my books was, I believe, 25,000. That's not all bad. And when a paperback writer reaches the point of bestsellerdom, you're talking 100,000 readers and up—way up! So you're beginning to acquire quite a lot of readers! And it's important to me that people read my books; I'm not writing in a vacuum. It's also not *that* important to me that my books be made into movies or hardcover novels.

But, on the other hand, I wouldn't fight film deals either.

J.N. WILLIAMSON

I feel that, for sheer writing, *Bid Time Return* is the best book I've written. I've created in a sense a whole society of people out there who responded not only to the film, but to the book, the music, everything. I feel very good about that. I feel extremely good about *What Dreams May Come* because I've had letters from people saying, "My mother was dying, and I let her read this book, and she faces her death now with peace." And I think no writer can do more than that.

RICHARD MATHESON

I've finally got the car I've always dreamed of. It's a Fleetwood Brougham, in white, with an interior the color of Joan Collins' toenails. Being an author, you lead such a solitary, monkish life. But as soon as I get onto the street, I'm immediately visible. You know the size of most of the cars in England—everyone's stuck to the windows like those suction-cup Garfields. It was Liberace who said, "It's awful being stared at, but *not* being stared at is worse!" The car is wonderfully inconvenient. You don't get much notice being a writer; it's not like being a motion picture star because they don't recognize your face. And several of the writers I know have vulgar cars.

GRAHAM MASTERTON

There is a level that I tend to get pigeon-holed as a horror writer. But, then again, anybody who knows anything about my body of work knows that isn't *all* I do. And *Sandman* isn't even particularly horror. So I can't really think of any way its [popular success] affected me adversely. It generates an interesting body of fans, 99% of whom are quite wonderful. And 1% of whom take it all a little too far and assume that I am privy to a body of wisdom denied to the commonality of mortals.

Now *that's* a little difficult to deal with. . . .

NEIL GAIMAN

Success is the result of being true to your voice, true to your identity, and true to what you're trying to accomplish. And having patience.

DAVID MORRELL

One of the big problems that new writers have, especially those whose star rises really quickly, is that they get the idea they're writing "art." Well, anybody who sits down to write "art" is deluding himself. I always use the same examples, and I don't care if they're now regarded as geniuses: Shakespeare didn't write "art," and neither did Charles Dickens. *They wrote to make a buck.* And to entertain their audience—so they could continue to write and make a buck. It just so happens that they *were* both geniuses, and their work has lasted. But nobody knew that at the time. The test of time is the only way to judge if anything is a classic.

Now I have things to say in my books—but it's all below the surface, and I don't set out with a conscious theme. I just set out to tell a story. That's *it*. If there's anything else in there, that's cool. If the reader gets it, that's great. If the reader sees something I didn't intend to put in there, that's *wonderful*. But the important thing is that they get to the end of it, and they don't feel that I've cheated them.

CHARLES L. GRANT

I do think that it's true that "if we give you enough rope you'll hang yourself." I think now I have enough rope so I can hang myself in Times Square at high noon with three network coverage. If I told somebody I wanted to rewrite The Bible in common prose, I could probably get six figures for it at this point. And that's the problem— I'm not saying that to be a hot shit or conceited or anything else. But for me, that's the problem.

STEPHEN KING

It only took ten years, seven unpublished novels, and a lot of blood later before I sold *The Wolfen*.

WHITLEY STRIEBER

There's a wonderful story I once heard about dear old Boris Karloff. In some interview, somebody one said to him, "Gee, Mr. Karloff, a wonderful, talented actor like yourself, with the range that you obviously have, it's a shame that you've been so horribly type-cast." Karloff looked at them in that kindly, gentle way that he had, and patted them on the hand and said, "Oh, no, no! I was never so grateful." And I am! It's helpful to be typecast like this; it's *nice*. I like being thought of as kind of spooky.

GAHAN WILSON

It depends on what kind of writer you want to be; what you're going to be satisfied with. I'm not talking money now. I'm talking about the size of the audience that will satisfy you. Will you be happy with a small audience, a middle-size one? If you're really serious about your writing, and have a view to impart that you think is important, then you're *never* going to be satisfied with the size of the audience you'll get as a mid-list genre writer.

If, however, you'd be happy to make a comfortable—though at times uncertain—living with a medium-size genre audience, then you will approach your career totally differently. You'll write smaller, less complex books. They might be brilliant books, you understand, but they'll be different because you'll be seeking a different niche. The problem is that some people say they'd be happy with that, then they discover they aren't happy when they're stuck in such a career.

I know many writers who have spent twenty years developing a fine genre reputation with which they are completely dissatisfied. They have done excellent, admirable work—and they're miserable. Now, after all these years, they're so typed, they can't escape the jail they've built for themselves. Publishers see them as writers with a limited audience, and they're never given the chance to do the broader work when they're ready for it.

It's wise to plan early on where you'd like to go, do serious self-analysis to determine what you want from a writing career. Now, I made the same mistake. When I began I thought I'd be comfortable as a straight genre writer. I just kept switching genres as my interests grew! I have since been fortunate that—with a great deal of effort—I have been able to break the chains of genre labeling, and do larger and more complex books. But it's very difficult, and very few people who develop straight genre reputations ever escape them.

DEAN KOONTZ

You've got to want the process of writing more than the achievement. The pleasure has got to be in the business of the writing, not the business of the publishing. If you spend the six months of writing a novel thinking about what it's going to look like on the bookshelves, you're not doing it right. A lot of fledgling writers that I've spoken to, if there's one pitfall they weren't aware of, is that the writing life was great—except for the bit about actually doing the writing. They *loved* the idea of being published, they *loved* the idea of going on TV talk shows; but if they could just get over this fucking business of actually doing the writing. If they could just get that bit over . . . !

CLIVE BARKER

I really don't know if it's now any more difficult to break in as a horror writer. It's *always* been difficult to get published. But now, in publishing, the tendency is for there to be "blockbusters" and everything else is left down at the bottom. It's really the same way with movies. If you're not one of these summer blockbusters making at least 100 million dollars at the box office—then you're nothing! You're out of the theaters in a week. It's the same way of thinking in the bookstores.

You go into any major bookstore, and you'll find shelf after shelf filled with the same bestselling authors. And then, maybe, you'll find one or two copies of books by people who are just as good, but are simply not as well known. They've basically been shut out of the game...

However, if someone does write a good novel, it's very likely that he or she will find a publisher for it, sooner or later. The fact is, if you write a *lousy* novel, the chances are equally good you'll find a publisher! Unfortunately, there are a great many editors who don't know the difference.

RICHARD LAYMON

[Fans] are the concrete evidence that you touch people's lives. Like the guy who called me and said, "Last year I had a leg amputated, and was in the hospital for that and related problems dealing with cancer for a period of several months. In the course of that time I lost my business, and my wife left me." And he told me, with his voice breaking, "The only thing that got me through that year, and made me want to go on, were two books of yours, *Strangers* and *Watchers*. Which were scary novels, but were filled with so much hope, and so much faith in human beings, that reading them repeatedly got me through times I don't know how I would have otherwise gotten through." That for me is what writing is all about. If something in your writing gives support to people in their lives, that's more than just entertainment—which is what we writers all struggle to do, to touch people. Entertainment is just a vehicle to reach them on a much deeper level.

Also, a woman wrote me and said, "My father is dying of cancer. He is the most wonderful father anyone could have had, and he's only in his fifties, with six months to live. I'm not articulate enough to say all the things I want to say when I speak at his funeral. There's a long passage in *Twilight Eyes* about how what we really fear is not our own death, but the deaths of those we love. Would it be possible for me if I could read that at his funeral service and reprint it in the program?" Man, you can't answer a letter like that fast enough! Something you've written has clearly touched someone on a deep, personal level, and speaks directly to their lives. *Those* are the moments when you think you're doing something worthwhile.

DEAN KOONTZ

CHAPTER FIVE

Going to the Movies

Although I've had success in novels, I sometimes think maybe I should no longer keep trying, because although they work out reasonably well, none of them have sold a lot. Maybe *Hell House* did. But their only value to me financially was that they sold as motion pictures. I suppose it's nice to have a couple of novels that people call "classics"—*The Shrinking Man* and *I Am Legend*—so obviously I'm going to keep on writing them. But I do feel that the film medium is a tremendously powerful one, if used properly. Of course, it is very rarely used properly.

RICHARD MATHESON

You know how movies are rewritten, and rewritten, and rewritten. Everything in a screenplay is conditional. Anything you write down is subject to almost infinite change. A screenplay is a blueprint for another activity—that activity will happen on the floor when you actually start to shoot the picture. At that point, another set of voices—quite different from the producers and the executive producers' voices you've already heard—enters the scenario.

There's the actor who feels a line could be improved or turned, the cameraman who has a different view of how the scene should be shot . . . it's a long list. Then, when the shooting is done, the voice of the editor, who can literally reorder the lines you've written on the page, and can make completely new sense of them. Or make complete nonsense of them. So a screenplay is a very tentative article.

With *Hellraiser II*, for example, when Peter Atkins and I had

originally beaten the story out, it made sense. But by the time it went through all those voices, by the time it actually reached the screen, it didn't make anything like as much sense as it should have done.
CLIVE BARKER

When I was growing up, I went to almost every movie that came around. I always liked the horror movies, but most of them weren't very good. Most of them were very disappointing, except for a couple that really knocked me out—like the original *Invasion of the Body Snatchers*. I also read about the Ed Gein story—which the book and movie *Psycho* were of course later based on—when I was about ten or twelve years old. I read my father's copy of a true crime magazine, and that really hit me. It appalled me, yet I then developed a life-long interest in finding out what makes these psychopaths tick.

When we decided to make *Night of the Living Dead*, I remember doing a lot of talking about how, whatever film we made, it needed to be realistic in the characters, and the plot needed to be believable, so that hopefully we would have some of the same kind of impact on the audience that *Invasion of the Body Snatchers* did. Another film that had a great impact on me was *Forbidden Planet* because it was just done so well. Remember that most films in the horror or sci-fi genres were just sloughed off—the fans would always go to these films full of hope that they would see something good—and their hopes were always dashed! Just the thought that it was so much better than the run of the mill sci-fi or horror film stayed with me. Those were among the films that showed that something good could be done in these genres.
JOHN RUSSO

I always say the same thing: you have to get around a film production, somehow. The best way is to work your way through the ranks, unless you get real lucky like me and go make an independent movie and it becomes a hit. Then you'll get a blank check. So I'll never discourage anybody from going out and trying to make a little movie. That's cool. But if you can't do that, if you don't have an uncle who will give you a couple of grand, you have to get around somebody else's production. That means getting to a city where there is state-of-the-art production activity. Now, that doesn't necessarily mean that they are making features, but somewhere there's an active PBS station, like Boston or Pittsburgh. Some place where you can meet the working professionals, get on the set, work for free if you have to, make relationships. That's exactly the way it works. It's all grapevine, and anyone who has the instinct and the talent and the dedication, will come and find work.

It comes down to those old values. One thing about a film production is that it must run efficiently; there is no room for dead wood. So somebody that hangs around by the coffee wagon won't get hired again, but somebody who is dedicated and works hard and really puts out will get noticed by the people that matter around there, and will get asked to come back again. I've never seen it fail, it's almost automatic. If you have that spark, if you've got what it takes, you'll work. It's as simple as that—there's nothing mysterious about it.

GEORGE A. ROMERO

I adapted John Saul's *Creature* for Universal. They were very happy with the script. When they decided to make it, they hired a director . . . who insisted on rewriting it, and ten months later, handed in a Gothic script. I guess he had turned it into an Edgar Allan Poe story or something. And they don't like his script, so they dropped it! And that's end of the project, as far as I can see. This sort of thing happens over and over again in this business.

When they turn out badly, usually the writer gets the blame.

RICHARD MATHESON

My friend Mick Garris and I wrote a screenplay that we sold to Joel Silver. Again, great excitement, and . . . then they brought in a very prominent director, but [someone who's] not much of a writer. And he undertook rewriting the entire screenplay, and what was a greenlighted picture became a red-lighted picture. And that was the end of the project—at least for now. So the director has the power to bring ruination to a project. Whenever you see a bad movie you may be looking at the catastrophic result of *one* guy that comes in at the eleventh hour and changes everything.

RICHARD CHRISTIAN MATHESON

Someday I expect to do novels. But directing takes a lot of energy, and this is a job to do while you're still young. I'll do novels later on, when I don't want to get up at four o'clock the morning, work with a cast and crew, or travel as much. But I became a screenwriter first because I was movie-crazy.

LARRY COHEN

The [Norman Bates] you saw in the movie that you saw was very different from the one in the book [that Robert Bloch wrote]. I invented a history for Norman Bates because it was just something that I needed to know to write the scenes that I wrote. I'll have a history for any character that I write about, and can talk for hours about a character you'll see for maybe ten minutes on the screen. As a matter of fact, I discussed one sequence with Hitchcock, telling him how I was building up the life that had turned Norman into a youth who could kill his mother, and Hitch was very fascinated by it and sorry that we weren't able to shoot it.

JOSEPH STEFANO

Usually it's referred to as "Steven Spielberg's *Duel*." I'm very fussy—when I write a script, I see it in my mind; I write it *exactly* as I envision it. And almost never does it come close at all to my expectations. Occasionally it does, or even exceeds my expectations, as it did in *Duel* or in *The Night Stalker* or in *The Morning After*, a movie for television I wrote about alcoholism. And a few others. Then I'm very happy. But in motion pictures, I can't think of a single one that bowled me over right from the start. After a while, you usually forget about your original vision, and you begin to judge the film on its own merits. Then you start to accept it. For a long time, I didn't like *The Incredible Shrinking Man*, but as time went by, I began to see how unusual it was for its period, and how really nicely done it is. So I began to appreciate it more. But that's just the way my mind works.

RICHARD MATHESON

[The film versions of *The Wolfen* and *The Hunger*] were both overblown; they were both done by people who thought the horror genre was simply a vehicle, and they were trying to do things that were more "important" than horror. In *Wolfen*, the director was interested in making a political statement. In *The Hunger*, the director was interested in making an "art" film. Someone told me who had been at a party in London where [director Tony] Scott had said, "*The Hunger* is not a horror film, it's an art film." And I thought, "It's a bomb. It's doomed." But if the directors had just been honest . . . it was the same way with the second version of *Cat People*. And *Ghost Story* was the same deal—the directors don't have any respect for the little man. Either the little man who made the pictures which are going to live forever, or the little man who watched them and went away, feeling somehow a kind of catharsis in himself for having been there.

WHITLEY STRIEBER

You fight battles in movies in ways you don't in books. There's only one real enemy in writing books, and that is your own entropy. Your own laziness. In movies, there are all kinds of enemies: lawyers, accountants, list-makers, the upper echelon of the studio sometimes—people who don't want to risk their jobs, people who don't want to support an original vision. There are compromises and intellectual mediocrities. There's a lot of these enemies in the studios—but there's a lot of them in every walk of life.

CLIVE BARKER

All I can say is what I wrote ain't what's up there on the screen! But I can tell you some of the reasons why the screenplay [for *The Howling II*] was so badly screwed up. First, I wrote a pretty straight movie version of my book for the producers. And they said, "Gee, this is nice, Gary, but we just got a bunch of money from some Spanish people, and they'd like a large percentage of the film to be shot in Spain." Of course the story took place in Los Angeles and Mexico, but I said, "Okay, I can do that." So I moved everything to Spain for some reason or another.

And then they said, "Oh, one more thing: Fernando Rey is a good buddy of the producer, and he'd like a part written for Rey." And I had no Fernando Rey character, but again I said, "Okay—what the hell? I'll write Fernando Rey in." So I did. I gave them another draft. And they said, "Gosh, Gary, this is nice, too, but you know what? The Spanish money just dropped out, and we're going to film in Yugoslavia." I had a book commitment by that time, so it was goodbye for me. They brought in another screenwriter, rewrote the script, took the production to Yugoslavia, ran out of money, spent about twelve dollars on special effects—filmed it mostly in the dark so nobody would notice—and that's the last I know about that one.

GARY BRANDNER

When it's a particular piece that I'm really in love with, that I'll direct. But I write so much; I write every day. When I have nothing to do, or am waiting for something to happen, I'll write. So by the end of the week, I've accumulated a stack of pages. And by the end of year, I have more scripts than I could ever possibly do myself. There are scripts I write that nobody likes, but eventually, sooner or later, most of them find a home.

LARRY COHEN

Another question that one is often asked is why have things like trucker movies and Westerns all gone away and horror is still there? It's because horror is very much deeper than those other [genres]. It's right there at the primal level of human existence and therefore it is immune to trends and cultural upheaval. It of course shifts, but it is immune to being eradicated unless by censorship.

DAVID CRONENBERG

I've been told that there must be at least forty variations on *Psycho*. And people who are not familiar with the original film—or the novel—find this all very innovative. But I think everything, to a certain degree, is developed from a writer's readings and association with other work. It's just a matter of degree there as to whether it constitutes a point of departure or inspiration, or just plagiarism.

ROBERT BLOCH

The nice thing about it is you get paid a whole lot of money for movie involvement. And they *do* pay well. I hear writers crying all the time about "They did this to my book, they did that to my book . . . !" Now that's fair, because changes are made. But nobody puts you in a hammerlock and says, "You gotta sell your book to Hollywood or we're going to kill you!" These producers are making a movie, and a movie is *not* a book. They try to do what they think will be successful, and if it isn't, then you can go out and get drunk, cry, raise hell, with the other writers.

But in the long run, you *did* sell it, so just mellow out and take it!

GARY BRANDNER

Anybody who wants to do what I'm doing—that is, write and direct motion pictures—first they've got to *write*. They've got to continually write, like I do. All the time. They've got to turn out some scripts. The easiest thing to do—of all the challenges to overcome—the easiest one is writing. If you can write something and someone reads it, they might very well make the picture. A director has a harder job: he has to have film, equipment; he's got to have a crew, got to have actors, got to have a script, locations. He's got to have a budget. A writer only needs a piece of paper. All it costs him is 120 sheets of paper. You can turn out a product at a negligible cost. So I would say if you have writing talent, then you should utilize it. If you don't have writing talent, then you have a problem. Then you've got to find somebody *else* who can write, team up with them, and hope to come up with something. If you're a producer, you find somebody who's written a script, and try and find a home for that script. You might try and tie them up with a director ... there's a lot of ways to do it. Writing is still the easiest way— *if* you have the talent.

LARRY COHEN

First let me say it's better to learn from a bad script then a good one. Because with a good screenplay, you're not going to know what makes it good when you're starting out. But with a bad script that gets produced, then you may have a chance to figure out what makes it work. I'm sure people could tell *Beetlejuice* hadn't been written by someone working in Hollywood, but there was something about the script that they liked, and they bought it. If your script is good, there is somebody somewhere who will read it.

MICHAEL McDOWELL

An awful lot of writers spend a great deal of time pursuing Hollywood, and while they're doing this they're ignoring writing their next novel. I figured out a long time ago it might be better to write a whole bunch of novels than go out and try to court Hollywood. My books are all out there. They're going to be out there for a long time to come. Somebody wants to make a movie out of one of 'em, that's fine with me.

RICHARD LAYMON

It's a question of having 2,000 elements to get into a screenplay, and only having 124 boxes in which to put these elements. And so, every box has to have a peg that is eight-sided, and every peg has to do double, triple, and quadruple-duty. Do you understand what I mean?

[Compared to writing a novel] these screenplays are exercises, and they have to be treated as exercises. It's wonderful when you can do the exercise, and then sneak in something on top of that. Putting something of yourself in it. Because when you're actually writing, working it out, so much of it can feel like choreography. And blocking. Getting your characters on, getting them to move about, getting them resolved. So it's not like writing a novel. It's as if I had 600 pages of a novel, and all the things I brought to that novel, all the aspects that I developed and tied on to it, that I suddenly had to do that in 115 pages. And not lose any of it in the translation. You also have to have a Hollywood audience in mind—not necessarily a film audience—but a Hollywood audience that ultimately judges you. This is not a negative comment because I work out here, but it is part of the system . . .

MICHAEL McDOWELL

You just have to be prepared to speak to your vision, even if it does not suit certain individuals, and know that when you make movies, you have to work with other people. You have to share your vision with others, and say: "Listen, come with me on this adventure." You hope to find producers sympathetic to that. You hope to find marketing people who will understand that vision. You hope to find actors and special effects people who will give their life's blood to make that happen. Most of the time you're disappointed.

CLIVE BARKER

When I was given the opportunity to write for the series [*Tales from the Darkside*]—which came about in a very strange way—I asked to see a sample script. I was given George Romero's script for the pilot episode. I looked at that, and I took it apart, and I imitated it. I put my story in its format, with the peaks in the same places, and figured out how long scenes were, and so forth. And it worked. I also got another script accepted because in this case it had one set and one actress. It was called "Answer Me" with Jean Marsh. But I enjoy the constraints. It's like working in a hot house, and forcing bulbs. Sometimes they bloom bigger and grander if you decrease the size of the pot.

MICHAEL McDOWELL

I was sick in bed one day with the flu. And a man called on the telephone and said, "Hello, my name is David Vogel and I'm the producer of *Tales from the Darkside*, a television show. Are you Michael McDowell?" And I said, "I am" He said, "I would like to buy your story "Slippage" for the show. You *are* Michael McDowell, the horror writer?" He waited for a response, and finally I said, "You have the wrong Michael McDowell, horror writer." I told him, "You want Michael Kube-McDowell." And he was so embarrassed, he said, "Well, uh, do *you* have anything?" So I said, "Yes, I do." And I didn't. So I went upstairs and I wrote something, real quick. And that was "Inside the Closet." I sent it to him, he bought it, and I ended up doing four episodes that same season.

MICHAEL McDOWELL

I have always believed that the whole area of imaginative movie-making, and imaginative fiction on the page, is in fact one territory. It isn't divided up neatly into science fiction, and horror fiction, and fantasy fiction. *Alien*, for example, is very clearly a horror movie. And it's very clearly a science fiction movie. They are *not* mutually exclusive genres. I would like to see more cross-fertilization between these areas than we've seen in the Eighties, when horror movies had only one thing on their mind: to make people jump and accomplish very little else. Where there was the occasional *frisson* because the soundtrack went quiet for a while, and then a loud sound came in and a guy with a machete appeared. I would like to see the movies embrace a more fantastical, and more imaginative, attitude to horror fiction. Any genre is the sum of the people who want to work in it; there's always been an audience for this kind of picture. There always will be.

CLIVE BARKER

I wouldn't want to make another *It's Alive* picture if there wasn't anything new to say. In each film, the story is more about the characters and less about the monster babies.

It's about the unusual and bizarre things that happen to us, that we don't *want* to happen to us. But they do. Peoples lives can be shattered, no matter how happy they may be. Your kids leave for school, and in the back of your mind, you're wondering if they will make it back in one piece. No matter how beautiful or sweet life is, there are always shadows lurking around the corner. And you're always saying, "It's not going to happen to us, it'll happen to somebody else's family." And my characters are basically nice people who find themselves in the middle of one of those awful situations.

LARRY COHEN

There's a mythology about directing. Everyone that you meet thinks they can write. They may not be convinced they can write brilliantly, but they're convinced they can *write*. Not everyone is convinced they can direct. Directing seems to bring out a lot more anxiety because there are technical aspects to it: knowing what lenses do, knowing how to light a scene. When you talk to people about this, it brings up a certain amount of apprehension. So the director has an incredible amount of mythological power, and that is why the system in Hollywood is set up this way—and why it's so out of whack. The director is the last person to come in to perceive and render the material. But it's crazy to bring in somebody literally a month before a production begins, who has nothing to do with it, and then have the power to wreck your screenplay, simply because that's the position of power that they're in.

But that's the system.

RICHARD CHRISTIAN MATHESON

Ultimately, the writing of the book, the successful reception of the book by readers, and the filming of the book—that's the whole process. But if the book doesn't sell, and the readers don't respond, then I feel like I've failed. Because the reader is as important as the writer in the creative mix. The reader is also a creator—a partner—and if you don't have a partnership, then you've failed somehow; you haven't done it right.

WHITLEY STRIEBER

If no other movie was ever made of my work, it would not break my heart. The book is the ultimate statement that I can make; it's the most intimate, the most confessional. Movies are fun because you can remake the story. But the book is not the movie, and the movie is not the book. The book is God—in the beginning was the Word, and the Word means the author. I've been driven more crazy by more people directing two movies than I have writing eleven books.

CLIVE BARKER

This is an absolutely true story—I will not add or dramatize it in any way—I'll simply tell it exactly as it happened. Producer Stan Sheptner called me up one day [in 1977] and says, "Look, I've got ABC interested in a new version of *The Mummy*. I'd like you to take a crack at scripting it. Do you know anything about the original movie?" And I said, "Are you kidding? The Karloff classic? I love that movie! It's *horror noir*." So he says, "Okay, come on over we'll talk about it." So we talked. He said the network executives wanted to bring it back to life via scientific means, and did I think that bombarding the tomb with gamma rays would do it?

And I said, "Sure, why the hell not!" So we have our meeting with ABC, and the network people tell us that pyramid power is "very big right now." (This was during the time that pyramid power was a big fad in this country, like the hula hoop once was.) Can we get pyramid power into this story? And I said, "Absolutely, I can give you pyramid power!" So they said, "Fine, fine! Get to work!" For weeks Stan and I plotted the story. One plotting session after another. Which is incredible, because usually I can wrap these things up in outline form in about a week. But Stan was always coming up with new ideas, and, in addition, the network was saying, "Give us more pyramid power!" And I told them, "I gave our hero a pyramid-shaped refrigerator, and in his backyard he reads under a pyramid shaped umbrella. But if you want more, I'll give you more."

Then the network executives say "We want a really mean, fast mummy. We don't want him drag-footing along like Karloff." So I say, "Fine. You got it. This guy will move like Mick Jagger."

"And he's gotta be *strong*," they tell us. So I devise a scene where the mummy tears a parking meter right out of the concrete and smashes it across the windshield of this cop car and the car goes across the street and smashes into a dry goods store. And the mummy skitters off down the street, slowly unraveling as he goes, still wrapped up in his mummy shroud after being brought back to life with the gamma rays. So the whole concept is getting worse and worse, and I'm starting to think, "How did I get ever get into this mess?" But I want to get paid for my efforts—I'm only getting $7,500 for this outline, and the real money is on the other end when I get a go ahead for the actual teleplay. So I convince myself to stick with it, because at that time, it would have been $25,000 for the script.

Finally, Stan and I go back to the network for the final meeting. The ABC executives tell us, "We love it! You've got pyramid power, the gamma rays, you've got a damn strong mummy, and you've got him moving fast. We loved the scene where he kills the blonde in the swimming pool and the cops find this little unwrapped piece of mummy shroud floating in the water. So . . . we have some good news and bad news for you." Stan and I are sitting there, and we say, "Fine. Give us the good news first." And the executives says, "You have a green light. It's a *go* for scripting." And I said, "That's great!" (I could see the $25,000 worth of sugar plums dancing in the air.) "What's the bad news?" "The bad news is that we want *one* more change." And I said, "Hey, no problem. I'm Mr. Change. You name it, I can handle it. What do you want me to do?"

"Drop the mummy."

There was this long silence in the office. Stan and I looked at each other, and I remember saying, "You want to do *King Kong* without the ape?"

And this executive says, "We don't *need* the mummy! All we need is the mummy's curse. After they enter the tomb in the first act, all of our characters die, one by one. At the end, there's this big question mark on the screen. Did the curse of the mummy destroy these people, or was it life itself which destroyed them?" The executive turns to me. "What do you think, Nolan?" And I said, "I think I'll leave." And I did. I walked out and that was that. Now you see how easy it is to go crazy out here in Hollywood. It's Alice down the rabbit hole. Madness personified.

WILLIAM F. NOLAN

CHAPTER SIX

Sex and Death and Other Unspeakable Concerns

I feel horror fiction is *very* erotic. People have written really brilliant essays on that subject. It's absolutely inherent in vampire material: the drinking of the blood, the taking of the victim; all of that is highly erotic. It's an echo of the sex act itself. Since the Middle Ages, people have referred to the orgasm as the "the little death." So the connections are there. But when I'm writing these novels, it's not thinking consciously about that: I'm just imagining I'm a vampire.
ANNE RICE

It's not always just the scares and gross-outs that people are responding to ... regardless of the genre, writers should be able to create a real world that readers can identify with and want to live in for a time through their imaginations.
RICHARD LAYMON

I don't believe it is a writer's mission to cater to the tastes—or lack of taste—of the supposedly jaded reader. I don't believe writers of horror fiction are engaged in a contest to see who can most nauseate these jaded readers, or present the most graphicly disgusting descriptions. The Romans started with simple chariot races and ended up trying to devise extreme and atrocious methods of torture and mass murder. I don't regard this as an improvement.
ROBERT BLOCH

Everybody talks about horror as if it always *has* to be scary. I'm always amused when I read reviews which say, "This provides the required amount of chills." Or "There aren't quite enough scares here." What the hell?! Are we writing just to make the reader wet his pants? That's a pretty dumb reason for writing a story! There's got to be more to it than that. What I'm concerned with is the other human emotions. There *are* other emotions other than fear.

Fear is a very easy emotion to evoke. All you do is pull a knife on somebody and hold it to their throat, and they're going to be scared. And you can do the literary equivalent of that a half a dozen ways per page.

It's easy to scare a reader.

It's easy to gross out a reader.

What *isn't* easy is to reach down inside the reader and hold the mirror up, and get to the more serious subjects that horror writing can reach, such as self-recognition. And by that I mean the monster being ourselves. My goal is to make the reader take a second look at himself. The way he thinks, the way he lives.

I'm not crusading, by any means. I'm just saying that there's more to my stories than just providing thrills. Or there should be.

CHET WILLIAMSON

I am firmly convinced that you can get more mileage out of directing the reader's imagination than laying everything out for them in such detail that nothing is left to their imagination.

I'm often given credit for incredibly realistic descriptions of people and places. The truth is, my descriptions are almost non-existent. What I do is describe a house as a "Victorian pile." And *everybody* has seen dozens of Victorian piles, and everyone has one that stands out in their mind, whether they remember it precisely or not. And they think I've described it, when actually I didn't—I just cued an image in their mind.

JOHN SAUL

I don't like to look at films that are trying to be more graphic, more violent than the last picture. But I realize there is a certain element of the audience, especially young teenagers, who go to these films because they're interested in the special effects and the make-up. Who want to know "How'd that guy's head came off?" or "How did they drive that nail through a guy's forehead?" This curiosity is nothing new—the *grand guignol* did this in France for years. It was a major attraction for this theater group to perform these horrific acts on stage. People would go to see it just to ask, "How did they do that? How could they chop somebody's head off right on the stage?" So I can understand how there's always been a certain market for that sort of thing.

It's just never been my idea of show business.

LARRY COHEN

I don't believe there can be such a thing as "bad taste." There can only be bad writing. You can have the most outrageous scene with the most extreme violence, and handle it in such way that it'll be extremely excruciating—but there'll be no blood. So I don't think there can be any bad taste in creating a scene, only bad writing in handling it.

ROBERT R. McCAMMON

Certainly there are some very talented writers who can handle the gore. I've enjoyed some "gross-out" fiction. But they do tend to be by writers who have something to say about people. And society. So in that sense it's worthwhile reading. But then there are those who miss the point entirely. They read a David Schow story, and all they see is the "red." So when they go to write their own horror story, all they carry over are the carnal aspects. But they don't have the style, they don't have the wit. They just don't have the chops.

All you get is a red mess.

F. PAUL WILSON

But certainly a [horror] story can be erotic. And it can be frighteningly erotic. And there can be strong hints of sadomasochism in it; it's simply a question of the intelligence of the writer and how he or she handles what they're doing.

GRAHAM MASTERTON

I don't try to go beyond any "limit" in particular; I try to approach what I'm doing in a particular project—in a particular scene—and to give it a twist. To write it in such a way that people have never encountered before.

There are writers out there—I know of a few and I've read a few—who pile on the gore. But it's not particularly creative, and a lot of talent is required to make it work. I do believe I have a knack for describing the horrible without belaboring the point.

JOHN FARRIS

I look at the violence [in my work] very closely, and play it back, frame by frame. If I am doing violence, then at that point—in my mind— I'm doing a movie. If I'm doing character, I'm doing a novel. And if I'm doing a description of something real, say of a highway—how it smells or feels or tastes—then I'm doing something slightly different again. It's an old trick, a simple trick—I think anyone who's worth anything as a writer does it—but you've got to engage the senses. *Every* sense.

I'm very careful to wrap the reader around in smells and touches and sights. I like the sense of touch—with violence particularly, I try to get that sense of touch. Of what it feels like for flesh to part. It is hot? Is it cold? I try to engage those senses; I just think that way. Especially when I'm writing scenes of violence I think that way in particular.

JACK KETCHUM

We have to make that distinction of what I consider to be horror, and what the exploitation filmmakers consider to be horror. In the types which exhibit a certain restraint, I think there is this catharsis that does come from within, because it's built up from within. It isn't shoved in one's face, a blood pie instead of a custard pie, the way it's done in so many of these other films. In that case, you're not achieving catharsis—you're merely catering to voyeurism. Sadistic voyeurism. But the basic premise which I always try to stress is that it isn't so much what's shown, but the *attitude* toward it.

If the evil is condoned, or is presented in an amoral fashion by those who would recoil in disgust from the use of the word "evil" and then they walk away from it, I think it's quite a different story. But if the attitude is there, and you take a moral position, then I think it's a positive and constructive thing. But the anti-hero, the man or woman whose most atrocious activities are condoned because he or she is "avenging" something, establishes a very dangerous premise. And it ultimately leads to the Ku Klux Klan, the Inquisition, you name it.

ROBERT BLOCH

There's very little difference in giving the reader an erection—and giving him an erection of the spine. There's *got* to be more to it than that.

CHET WILLIAMSON

I once had a fan letter from a woman in Montana about *Night Songs*. She told me she enjoyed the book, but she deplored the explicit violence in it. There is *no explicit violence in the book*. She specifically mentioned one scene where a cop is sitting in a car, and Tess Mayfair, the woman from the boarding house comes up, and she reaches in the car and struggles with him—and she pulls off his arm. That's all I said: she pulls off his arm. Period. She mentioned that scene specifically because of all the blood and gore. I did not mention the word blood *once*. But the way I did it I guess must have been right because she filled it all in.

That's the best way do to it, I think.

CHARLES L. GRANT

It's not the tradition of the literature to show it all to the reader. The tales that have lasted all this time, that have become timeless in many instances, are the stories and novels that make *us* go to work as well. Make the reader bring his own subjective bag of fears and imagination into the mix. That's when the genre really works.

THOMAS F. MONTELEONE

If you just want butchery, you might as well go along and visit your local meat counter. It's about as frightening as that. And, it seems to me, that those writers who are becoming really successful at developing this genre are those who are exploring ways of making you *frightened* rather than ways of making you disgusted. Anybody can write a "meat story." You can write a factual piece describing a liposuction operation and that would be sufficiently disgusting. Anybody can do that, and it's not clever or impressive. And it doesn't take the genre anywhere.

GRAHAM MASTERTON

I think the average citizen doesn't really want a hardcore pukebag brand of horror. In a way, neither do I. I think the main thing about horror is that it should be fun. I don't like to read stories which are actually *upsetting*. Real life is upsetting. I think that reading a horror novel should be a trip to the funhouse, not the charnel house. I don't want to feel like I'm taking a tour through Auschwitz. I want to be scared, but I want it to be that fun kind of scare. That carnival kind. You *know* it's make-believe. When I'm writing, I want to frighten you, and sometimes gross you out, but I don't want you to feel as if I'm putting it to you in a torture chamber.

RICHARD LAYMON

Horror, perversity, and tragedy are just as much elements of supply and demand as apple chips and Elmo dolls. The market will always be provided with what it wants. That's why people rubberneck at car wrecks, that's why people rent *Atrocities* and *Faces of Death* at the local video store, and why they stare at Time and Newsweek photos of airplane crash victims naked and bloated with putrefaction as they're lifted onto Coast Guard graveships. Moreover, that's why Time and Newsweek *made damn sure* those awful pictures were there.

It's the same reason why people turn on "Geraldo" and "Jerry Springer" every day, because they *want* to see those crack moms, they *want* to see those pre-teen prostitutes and their needlemarks. They *want* to see the little girl with two heads, the Klan, the braggart "roofie" dealers, the gang-rape victims, and the woman with no arms and legs. As long as the "market" keeps begging for more, the "producers" will keep supplying it.

Hence, as the world gets sicker and sicker, so does its literature, because literature must always reflect the peripheries of reality.

EDWARD LEE

I want to make one important point. I'm not rigid in my tastes. I can appreciate violence—even overt violence—if it's coupled with really good characterizations, fine stylistic writing, and it's by someone who knows what he or she is doing. A good example would be Joe R. Lansdale's *The Nightrunners*. But most writers just don't know how to handle violence. They think if they nail a woman to a cross, that will do it. With crude, graphic gore you very quickly reach a point of saturation; you're soon looking for something with more depth to it, and I believe that's where the better writers are going to be coming in and staying with us, whether in books or on the screen. I like to think I'm one of them.

WILLIAM F. NOLAN

I really believe this: the most powerful books—not necessarily mine—are the ones which force the reader to use his imagination. Because there is nothing more powerful than the reader's imagination.

Writers who spell it all out—let it be the sex act or, more specifically, violence—are cheating the reader.

I think it's an insult to the reader's intelligence and imagination to spell it all out. But as Ramsey Campbell has said, *everybody's* imagination is under attack because television doesn't permit us to have an imagination. Good films always do. But the splatter films are a lot like television: it's quick scenes, punch go, punch go, with no room to think.

But when you're sitting down to enjoy yourself with a good book—or a good film—explicitness is lazy writing. I really think it is. They don't know how to suggest it, so they spell it out. It's a lot easier to spell something out than it is to suggest it. Let the *reader* fill in the rest! It has a greater impact than a whole paragraph describing entrails one by one.

CHARLES L. GRANT

I can tell you that in my pictures the violence is usually committed by a monster baby or a killer ice cream or a dragon—it's hardly relevant to the kind of violence you find in real life. I don't see how anybody could be affected by it; the violence in my films is so extreme—so beyond the norm. I don't make these films to portray intensely realistic beatings or intensely realistic tortures. I think films that do are basically sick, because they cater to the basest elements in human nature. I couldn't make that kind of film. I know I couldn't make a *Friday the 13th*. Unless there's a reason for the violence; to explore it seriously. But to have it gratuitously put there, simply to parade one vicious act following another, trying to outdo yourself with more blood in each scene, that's just sadism.

Even so, I don't think movie violence has too much of a relationship with reality. Because we've all seen a million movie fights. You see them on every television show, night after night. And once in a great while, you'll actually see a real fight, in a restaurant or in the street. And people don't fight in real life the way they do in the movies. It's not like it—*at all*. It's a different world—it's a different reality. What I'm saying is that people are not numbed out by the violence they see in the movies or on television. They know the difference.

LARRY COHEN

What I think the reader is looking for is the rollercoaster ride. They want to be *scared out of their wits*—and I think there's a big difference between scaring someone and grossing them out.

I enjoy international spy thrillers, and what I enjoy is the thrill of the chase. I'm not interested in reading about how someone dies; I'm interested in the vicarious thrill of being in that dangerous situation and *just* squeaking out of it. What people are looking for in a thriller is *tension*. There are a lot of writers out there who seem incapable of coming up with genuine psychological tension, but they certainly can go rambling on describing sex and violence. Which I believe is the cheap or lazy way out.

JOHN SAUL

New writers will also make the mistake of trying to "go for the gross-out" before they have worked up to the right psychological mood; they haven't created the atmosphere or the dramatic tension necessary to pull it off. What good writing is, when you boil it down (and it can be horror or suspense or science fiction or a love story): there has to be dramatic tension. You have to have people that are in conflict with themselves or with their adversary or their fears—whatever it is. The writer has to learn how to create that sense of "unease." That tension. Then, if there's a necessary gross-out, it works.

But most splatterpunk stories were ineffective for that very reason. Few bothered to set up any real dramatic tension between their characters. They were just going for the gross-out, and that gets very old very quickly. There's no mystery, there's no intrigue.

Nothing to anticipate.

I think one of the most important elements in writing horror and dark suspense is learning how to control what the reader anticipates. I mean, just the titles of "The Black Cat" and "The Pit and the Pendulum." Even just those titles make you anticipate something . . . *what could it be?*! New writers tend to undercut themselves; they forget about the power of suggestion.

THOMAS F. MONTELEONE

I have a great rejection slip from a literary agent. The first time I ever sent out a novel—one that's never been published, by the way—I got back a letter from this old, established agency saying, "The book shows a lot of talent, and we wish you success with it elsewhere, but we found it was too sadistic in subject matter and don't think we could handle it."

I framed that letter.

RICHARD LAYMON

You can write about *anything* if you write well. There's no problem with subject matter; it's just if the writer is skillful enough to carry it off without merely making it an exercise in gut throwing.
CHET WILLIAMSON

It's all in how you approach the material. In *Son of the Endless Night* I had a sex scene between a twelve-year-old girl and the protagonist, which could be interpreted as pretty gamey. But one of the keys to the scene is that she's *not human*, which some critics seem to overlook. Also, at that point in the novel I needed to get about as far down into the depths of degradation and evil as it is possible to go. In the thousands of horror stories that have been published, how many scenes truly make the reader's skin crawl?

We've had an abundance of things crawling out from under beds and popping out of closets. Even though my novel dealt with supernatural themes, I had to be very careful and choosy about graphically illustrating the point I wanted to make. No way to try to handle the scene "tastefully." So I did not. It was about as pornographic as you can find in fiction. I haven't had too much feedback on it; a couple of fellow authors thought I really had gone too far. They're right!
JOHN FARRIS

For instance, it's a known fact that in most instances of a violent death, the bowels let go. You don't want to put that in every time, because in a way it steals focus, and you have to deal with it, and by then it's already taken up more room in the reader's mind than you want. So that's self-censorship, in a way. But it's also a choice, a choice of detail.
MICHAEL McDOWELL

But it's funny—in terms of taste and what you should be allowed to do. I find that the one thing above all else which distinguishes the modern horror novel from what went before—in virtually every recent novel I've read—is that whenever a character is terrified, he or she immediately proceeds to wet his or her pants. And this seems to be the big "breakthrough" that modern horror has achieved. I'm thinking seriously of writing a novel about a small town, isolated, where you can tell that something has gone terribly wrong . . . because everyone is walking around with wet pants.
LES DANIELS

A lot of times, less is more. A lot of times, to create the anticipatory suspicion of a fear or horrible event is far more powerful than describing the actual incident.

THOMAS F. MONTELEONE

I'm certainly not afraid to show things to the extent that I believe horror films are cathartic. In the old Greek sense of catharsis, which is to say you go in and become involved with the character. And you are in one sense purged of your own anxieties by being involved in someone else's. I believe that to be graphic is to allow the audience their catharsis.

I once saw a very good horror movie on television called *Don't Look Now*, and the whole storyline is an anticipation of the death of the character played by Donald Sutherland. And the film was winding tighter and tighter and tighter, and then on the TV version that I saw, *they don't show you his death*. Now that's enough to make somebody run out and kill! Now to show it—to deny it to the audience—is really bad, I think. The whole film is heading toward that cathartic moment when he's killed. It's a strange moment, and it's sad, and it's terrifying. *But you need it.* And not to have it is totally frustrating.

DAVID CRONENBERG

I'm not particularly fond of long scenes of bloodshed; how many ways can you really do it, anyway? When I get into violence—something that's really terrible—I want it to be memorable. Because I can bring considerable power to bear on just such a situation, I do. I want the reader shaken and helpless not to continue reading. I don't pull any punches, but I don't look for opportunities just to gross people out.

JOHN FARRIS

The whole rationale behind *Off Season* was that I had never read a book that looked at violence so closely, and with such an unflinching eye, as some of the movies I had seen. Like *Last House on the Left*, *Night of the Living Dead*, and *Texas Chainsaw Massacre*. That's when I thought, "Well, here's a niche. And I can fill it." Then I came up with the idea of doing the book in a form that really harkened back to Jim Bishop's *The Day Christ Died*—which gives you a blow by blow description of what's happening every moment. Hence, the actual times of day make up the chapters. Since then, to varying degrees, I've kept that notion: "Let's go look at our subject up close and personal."

My personal experience with violence has been limited—only one major car crash. But it was odd to me how slow time went—it happened like that [snaps fingers]—but I felt like it was going on forever. While the car was rolling, I thought it was going on forever. So I want to try and capture that minutiae of experience with anything that's violent.

JACK KETCHUM

Regarding the so-called new-extremism in horror, readers and critics ask me, "Where does it stop? How much farther can it go?" I answer the question with a question: *How far can mankind's capacity for atrocity go?*

Fiction provides a metaphoric mirror to our times. And, as the Twentieth Century draws to a close, the reflection grows more unspeakable, pathological, and appalling. Hence, so does horror fiction. What we see in the mirror for the year 2000 and beyond can only be worse.

EDWARD LEE

There's really nothing you can do on the screen today that I would do with *Psycho* to make it any better. It was never intended to be what later became "slasher movies." It was always a psychological study of a very strange case, and I always dealt with it that way. I don't feel that adding a lot of very explicit violence or sex [in the sequels] changes the movie very much. I don't know what you could add to *Psycho* that would increase the intensity of it.

JOSEPH STEFANO

. . . Horror and sensuality have *always* been linked. Good horror writing is almost always sensuous writing because the threat posed in horror fiction is usually a veiled erotic threat. But if you go back to your earliest horror stories in English, there's always a tremendous emphasis on mood, and atmosphere, and the response of the physical body to the menace. Vampire fiction in particular is always sensuous, so there's no problem really. I mean, horror writers are almost always dealing in atmosphere and suggestion . . . *suggestion*. Confusion of the senses, confusion of the mind to overwhelming physical responses. That's part and parcel of the genre.

With me, there's no method. Writing to me *is* sensuality. It is talking about the assault on the senses, and the effect on the individual. You either do that naturally, or you don't do it. You can't school yourself necessarily in doing that. The most you can do as a writer is stand back from your material and say, "What have I left out? What was I feeling physically? What textual details are missing?" But there can be some wonderful writing with no textual details. You just have to go with whatever way it goes.

You can read just a few pages of Stephen King and can see that he's a very sensuous writer. It's the way he perceives the world, how a screen door closing sounds, or the flavor of a chocolate bar or a hamburger or whatever—it's all in there. *But it's in there because that's what King notices.* You may notice something else entirely from your own perspective. The main thing is to immerse yourself in the material, and reach for the intensity.

Again, go where the intensity is, go where the pleasure is,

Go where the pain is. Go for the passion. Do that honestly, and the rest will fall into place.

ANNE RICE

I try to do what Hitchcock did in his films. I will suggest, and in effect cut away—as he would do with a camera, but in this case verbally—and let the rest be imagined by the audience and/or the reader. I think it's much more effective than to just do a graphic, detailed description, which is the equivalent of showing graphic violence on the screen.

ROBERT BLOCH

I *like* to be frightened. I *don't* like to be revolted. I don't enjoy reading a "splatterpunk" story about a woman being nailed to a cross, about exactly how the nails are being pounded through her breasts. In the fright genre you can do a great deal with indirection rather than by desensitizing the audience with overtly graphic, violent acts of horror. In [writing] *Trilogy of Terror II* I only describe the legs of the victim sticking out of the bathtub. We don't have to see the cut throat. It's enough for the coroner to say, "Her throat was cut straight across." We don't have to see it—and we especially don't have to see the throat actually being cut. The imagination can create greater horrors than we can ever show on the screen or in a book.

As a writer, I don't give my readers or viewers any more information than they need. What is primary in creating true horror is the mood and the build up. And the suspense. It *isn't* the ax in the brain

with the blood running down into the guy's mouth and his eyeballs popping out. I prefer to let the reader and the viewer create the ultimate horrors within their minds. The human mind can conjure up far greater terrors than any set designer. Charles Beaumont called it "the fiend in you."
WILLIAM F. NOLAN

To get the emotional response I'm after, I believe the violence is necessary, depending on the story. I've always loved horror, and I'm kind of a "genre mixer," and one of the things I greatly enjoy doing in a story is replacing catharsis with horror. The way it is in movies and most adventure comics, catharsis is essentially a very satisfying, very happy conclusion: the Death Star blows up, or whatever. Making that moment terrifying is something I like to play with, so it no longer leaves you feeling all is right with the world.
FRANK MILLER

I think there's a point when being graphic is necessary. And it's a totally subjective matter as to how much is just right. I think there's a point where you want to say, "This is *really* happening."
And you've got to say, "This is *how* it's happening."
DAVID CRONENBERG

I did pull out *all* the stops when I wrote my story for the anthology *The Book of the Dead*. But I think this is a factor that horror writers have do deal with: if you want to try for major success, you can't be too "far out." To have that "blockbuster mainstream" novel, you have to temper the nastiness, gore, sex, sadism—all that fun stuff!
So I've been going more in the direction of toning myself down. I still try to come up with some real nasty material, but I have been self-censoring myself a little bit lately. It's not just me, though. I've seen this trend going on with most horror writers whose careers I've been following: a *lot* of them start off real gritty, and then taper off as time goes by. I don't think it's because they're mellowing with age. I think it's because they have an eye on the marketplace, and they're looking for a wider audience.
RICHARD LAYMON

I never cared for the blood and gore, though *Suffer The Children* was my goriest. And I also think it's much more of a challenge to instill a sense of terror, rather than simply to try to shock the reader. I think *that* is absolutely the cheapest thrill in the world.

To me, if you can't think up a good plot, then you go about tearing people to shreds? I think it's revolting. If I pick up a book and see that's what the author is doing, I don't bother to buy it. If you can't think up a plot that's terrifying, if you can't dream up something that is truly frightening rather than just disgusting, you should go get an honest job. Basically, all it is is pornography.

JOHN SAUL

When you get into movies where there are seven or eight young people at a mountain cabin, and one by one they're getting killed, it almost becomes a sport. And it no longer has anything to do with character—or caring.

It becomes a game. You're not being moved by death anymore—or loss or grief—you're [just] kind of fascinated by how they came up with that new idea [of gruesomely killing off a character].

JOSEPH STEFANO

I certainly don't say, "This is too gruesome." I don't often say, "This isn't gruesome enough!" because I usually hit it first time around, as far as I'm concerned. I'm much more likely to think to myself, "Oh, that's hideous!! My God! Let's put *that* in!" I get very delighted when I create something that's pretty terrible.

RAMSEY CAMPBELL

My policy is, "Nothing succeeds like excess."

There is *nothing* one shouldn't be allowed to do in fiction. But in practice, it's worked out in strange ways. I often think I'm writing something that's outrageous and offensive because I'm dwelling on it at such length. It may take me an hour to write a paragraph that someone else will read in seven seconds. I haven't had too much trouble with publishers, though. I *like* lurid, flamboyant, melodramatic horror. It's great fun.

Maybe in the screenplays I've written that haven't been produced, what I was doing would have been considered excessive. Not because it was really any different, but people reading books sometimes just glibly pass over things that, if they actually saw them, would be too outrageous. But I'm in favor of outlandishness and bad taste.

LES DANIELS

It's a major preoccupation of mine. I've always felt it's something that horror fiction—and let's use the more collective term *fantastique*—generally doesn't address as well as it should. Sex in horror fiction and movies doesn't tend to be the subject of the work as much as it is light relief between the darker goings-on. Or maybe you're just setting up the characters to be murdered in their beds, which again doesn't seem terribly interesting.

But sex figures greatly in our sense of ourselves, and in our sense of how we physically appear in the world. Sex affects what our bodies do, how they change, how vulnerable they are. It affects our sense of personal ambition, and how much we want to achieve in terms of our sexual lives. It certainly affects what our sense of nightmarish and scary is, because there are so many elements in the sexual process where we relinquish control. And loss of control, for most people most of the time, is a *very* scary notion. Sexual fever is essentially a place where reason is suspended.

One of the things I love about art is you can employ reason and emotions simultaneously. The best fiction pricks the emotions: makes you laugh, cry. Be scared. And at the same time it stimulates the intellect.

CLIVE BARKER

In *Reborn* there's a scene where a little boy is horribly mutilated, but he can't really die. The scene in which the priest goes into the house and finds him . . . I really loved this little kid. But I had to do something awful to him—because the whole idea was to break the priest. So something awful *had* to be done to someone he cared about. Something that would be enough to drive him from his faith. But I had an aversive reaction to my keyboard. I'd type a few words. Then I'd get up and wander around the room. Then come back and type a few more. But I just did *not* want to write this scene. But—it had to be done. It was for [the good of] the story. It wasn't for the effect on the reader—it was for the effect it would have on the character. So I forced myself to do it.

Rarely has there ever been anything else like that that I had such a strong reaction to, but I did not do this to gross out the reader. I did it to *gross out the character*. That should be the guideline a writer should use: "Are you doing this just to get a gut reaction; to push a button in the reader? And if so, do you have a good reason for pushing that button?" If you're doing it just to shove the reader's nose in it,

then you're just playing with yourself. You *have* to have a story-based or character-based reason. Otherwise it's nothing but making a mess.
F. PAUL WILSON

Horror writers are now like that Bohemian society in Paris in 1920's, where everybody had their own style of art, and their own philosophy about art. This one was experimenting in Cubism, and this one in Naturalism. . . . But what they were really all talking about was the same thing—they were really talking about Art. So it doesn't matter whether we talk today about "quiet horror" or "splatterpunks" because there's great horror within all these voices. And I know I'm trying to sound diplomatic, but I'm not: I enjoy all these spectrums, and there's room for all of them.

So to say "Well, there should only be quiet horror, no blood and guts" or that it should be the other way around, diminishes the field. Diminishes the force of horror itself. It may be that horror is forever undefinable. It will always have these different voices and moods, and there may be no way to tame *or* define it. And that may be one of the great powers of horror fiction.
ROBERT R. McCAMMON

It's very easy to offend—but it's not easy to offend deeply.
JOE R. LANSDALE

CHAPTER SEVEN

Censored

I cannot believe anyone would be injured by reading. Reading presupposes literature, and literature presupposes rational thinking. Reading about violence is not going to incite violence; reading about sex is not going to incite sex. I don't believe in censorship of any sort—*any sort.* I would go to see a movie that had anything in it—I think the ratings should be gone. I don't think there should be any censorship whatsoever. I don't think anything should be kept from anybody who wants to see it. So I don't think there should be any limits on the amount of violence shown on the screen, or written about in books. That's categorical.

MICHAEL McDOWELL

With the exception of *The Serpent and the Rainbow*, which I imagine was regarded as a love story or a political thriller or something, *all* of my films have been censored in a very disturbing way. Especially the last three or four films. Even though I've been scrupulous in not dwelling on violence, I have been censored for *intensity.* That just strikes me as terrifying. Because what they are saying is that it doesn't matter whether you have a bloody scene or not, it doesn't matter if there are lopped off limbs or not, what matters is that I'm simply too intense. Therefore I've been told that this very genre must be limited in its intent, which *is* to *be* intense! It's as if we're working in some kind of emotional ghetto, where we're allowed to kill each other, but just not allowed to feel anything about it. *Shocker*, for example, was censored in twelve separate sequences. Scenes that were not necessarily bloody, but judged too intense. It just leaves me feeling like there is simply not the freedom there that I need myself at the level that I want to make an expression. It's extremely frustrating, because I feel that the *Shocker* out now is *not* where Wes Craven is in the Nineties. It's simply the version that they've *allowed* to be out.

I am a responsible adult. I think all the time while making a film, "Would this damage a child emotionally? Is this violence just for prurient interests?" I really try to avoid that, to be just, to be accurate, to be graphic for only as long as I need to be. But that doesn't seem to be important to these people at all.

Once you've rated the movie, as far as cutting scenes out of it, I think it's a shame. You should leave that up to the filmmaker. If he's a good filmmaker he can determine how long to hold a shot of a bloodied head, or whatever. Just to get the desired effect, and then move on. There's no reason to dwell on it, because as I said, the imagination can do so much more. But I think it's a shame the way the MPAA goes about hacking up films, and the filmmakers have to bring their films back three and four times before the board. And at the end of it, there's nothing left.

WES CRAVEN

David Cronenberg has said a number of times that, "When I'm working as an artist, I have no responsibilities. It is the responsibility of the artist to be irresponsible." I think there's great truth in that. However, besides being an artist, I'm also a parent. And there are certain movies or programs I have told my young kids they can watch when they're older. But I find ways of exposing them to their interest in that material. I do not deny my kids access to any book that is in my home. I do not consider books dangerous.

STEPHEN R. BISSETTE

I don't believe in censorship in any form. I think there's room for the "splatterpunks" as well as the so-called "quiet horror" in the genre. Personally, I don't happen to like splattering gore, on a printed page or on the screen. I don't approve of it, but that doesn't mean I'm trying to stop it. I just don't want to have anything to do with it. I've never written a *Friday the 13th*-type film. And I never will.

To me, that kind of horror desensitizes people, instead of frightening them. It's not true horror, it's revulsion. I call it the "vomit bag school." The ax in the brain, and squashed guts in your dinner plate.

I think it works against the very principles that I love about horror on the screen and in print.
WILLIAM F. NOLAN

You certainly can't shoot a film thinking about the censors. That's no way to run any creative endeavor. But, it's equally no use for me to spend a day shooting a piece of special effects, if I know full well it's not going to find its way onto the screen. So what I try to do is find ways of making the material work so that the MPAA will look at the material and realize that all the material is dramatically justified.

Of course they're going to find some tough material in my pictures, and in my choice of subject matter. There's no way that they're not going to find stuff they're going to choke over! What I'm saying is that when I go on the floor in the morning to shoot a scene, I'm not thinking of the MPAA—it's a useless endeavor. What they may be believing in today, they may disbelieve tomorrow. Certain areas of censorship come in and out of vogue. There are all kinds of areas which are subject to change, and I think they are a reflection of social pressures, and to some extent, political pressures.
CLIVE BARKER

Comics are particularly sensitive to censorship.

For example, someone who is confronted with the most *explicit* Clive Barker fiction still has to READ the page. What you are looking at is a page of typeset which is, in and of itself, completely inoffensive until it is actually read and engaged with. It's almost identical in appearance to any other page of text you could point to—such as a cookbook. But with horror comics, the underground comics, or any comics that are adult in nature, the viewer is immediately confronted with an *image*. And that image is easy to take out of context. That image is easy to misinterpret. That image may have a shock impact that is completely secondary to the narrative context it exists within. It's identical to, say, taking three frames of Sam Peckinpah's classic *The Wild Bunch* and making it look like it's just another Hershell Gordon Lewis gore movie. So comics have always been particularly easy prey for the censor.
STEPHEN R. BISSETTE

There was one story I decided not to write [for *The Sandman* series]. It would have been sort of a little complement to "Dream of A

Thousand Cats." It would have been a story about fetal dreams. It would have made a lovely story. Had it only been published in England, where abortion is not really a issue, I would have quite happily written it with no problems. But I chose not to write it, because I suddenly thought there would be some fifteen-year-old girl who's been raped and wants an abortion. And somebody would come up to her and show that story, and say, "How can you even *think* of getting an abortion after you read that story?" So I decided not to write it, which in a way tears me apart.

I know I had enough people come up to me and say that *Sandman* #8 got them over the death of their child, or the death of a best friend or someone like that. But you know that your stories *can* change people's minds, and hearts. So that was a case in which I decided to censor myself; I didn't want to be responsible for the consequences of a living soul.

NEIL GAIMAN

I don't censor myself at all when I write. I think as soon as you do that, you're finished.

DAVID CRONENBERG

Let's not forget censorship is a business. People make their living being censors . . . Jack Valenti has made a career by being a censor. It always fascinates me how often people who make their living as censors must say, "I am *not* a censor." Well, their hands on, day to day living is based on forcing writers, filmmakers, artists, musicians, and others to somehow alter their work to fit into categories they as censors have designed.

Now, these are people who tell us that exposure to these thoughts, images, words, sounds, will somehow be "dangerous" to us. That they're "not healthy" for us. And yet they make their living on a daily basis exposing themselves to words, images, sounds, thoughts that they are telling *us* are dangerous! If there was any truth at all to what the censorship industry has been ramming down our throat for at least two centuries now, today's censors would be the first ones out there on water towers shooting us down with submachine guns!

That's *not* the case. Which to me puts the lie to everything they have to tell us. These censors are not superheroes. These are not people graced with extraordinary powers of perception; they're just human beings who somehow claim they can digest this toxic material and then rescue us from its odious impact. While it has no impact whatsoever on them.

I don't buy it. I never have, I never will.

STEPHEN R. BISSETTE

Our culture has been enriched throughout history by dark dreamers. Re-envisioning, reforming, re-formulating images and ideas that have been part of the oral—and later the written—tradition in our culture since its instigation. If we were writing safe fiction, we wouldn't be interested in this process. But we're *not* writing "safe" fiction, at our best. We're writing a fiction which *is* confrontational. Which *is* dangerous. If *fantastique* fiction were indeed as "escapist" and "negligible" as many of the critics believe, one wonders why there are some critics who will raise their voices in disgust at it. If it's so harmless, why even bother to condemn it?

CLIVE BARKER

CHAPTER EIGHT

Personal Fears and Practical Philosophies

I'm a teller of tales in a time when tales are not being told. People react to my ability to work with metaphor. I'm very fortunate that God created me genetically able to take separate things and put them together and make a new metaphor out of them. And certain of my stories are such amazing metaphors that I look at them myself and say, "Where the hell did *that* come from?" It's a combination of what I was born with, and what I became, out of a fantastic curiousity in very many fields. And all this "junk"—this fabulous junk!—has gone into my head and comes out of my ears and my fingertips. I think people react to my childlike explosion. You see, I've remained the same person I was when I was a kid, and began to write. They react to this enthusiasm.

Even as I speak to you, I name my loves, and that's what you're reacting to: the ability to love life, and being alive, remains a *vital* concern. What I'm saying to people is, for God's sake, run out and *grab* things, and stuff them in your eyeballs, and up your nose and in your mouth. And go to the library and climb the stacks and *jump off*!!! It's a very primitive thing that's never changed in me.

Ray Bradbury

I call it the "Hitchcock perspective." Which is: "Something can *always* go bad." Alfred Hitchcock's thesis was that you could be leading your normal life, and by one little chance of fate, you can be plunged into a nightmare. A classic example is *North by Northwest*, where Cary Grant happens to get up the same time someone else's name is called for a message, and that's the basis for the whole movie. Or *Psycho*—if you pull off the road and stop at the wrong motel, you're going to end up being cut up by Norman Bates.

I view the world as a dangerous place. All the time. Especially in terms of my wife and my children, which probably makes me overly concerned for their safety. But the plus side, for those of us who write horror, is that you never run out of things to be scared of . . . !

MATTHEW J. COSTELLO

I tell stories which are effective to me in terms of hope. But then someone else might want to tell a story in terms of hopelessness. But my key word *is* hope; I think there's hope in any situation. And that's what motivates my characters to do what they do, because they think "There's a way out of this mess . . . " or "There's a way I can transform myself personally. . . . " Again, one voice may want to deal with horror from this perspective, while another may want to focus on the darkness. I have different tones in my stories, and hope is not always the right tone, but the element of hope is in most of my work.

ROBERT R. McCAMMON

I think horror writers evolve from undergoing trauma in childhood and draw upon their own fears in their adult careers. A competent writer can, by definition, usually fake almost any style in any genre, but the results are patently imitation unless there's an emotional involvement. As for scaring the reader, it obviously depends on just who the reader happens to be. Most eight-year-old kids tend to scare somewhat easier than, let us say for an example, Stephen King. In fact, I'd venture that most eight-year-old kids scare even more easily than *I* do.

ROBERT BLOCH

When I'm writing I don't think in terms of category. I just write a book because the idea seizes me and it sounds like it's going to be fun. Afterwards, however, you do have to define it in terms of the publisher having to market it. I guess horror is the closest you can come in defining my work. I used to think of them as "novels of suspense," especially *A Kiss Before Dying*. But the others do go beyond suspense because there's an element of fantasy, an element of unreal-

ity, and [to call them] "thrillers" doesn't quite do it somehow. So I guess I do write "horror novels."
IRA LEVIN

I can't speak for anybody else, but for me, it's getting in touch with those things that are inside myself that I would like to purge. That's *it*. Being in touch with those primal things in myself and not being afraid to realize them in the sense that I'm making them into stories and into images. A lot of people say when they meet me that "You're not what I expected!" I supposed they figure I'm going to be a raving maniac. Or a very melancholy figure.
DAVID CRONENBERG

I'll tell you what one of the strongest fears is that runs through my books. When you're a father, and a parent, and a husband, and a lover, you have very strong protective feelings about your family. I've been asked about the novels I write in the first person; not many horror novels are written in the first person because you give the game away right from the beginning—that the hero is going to survive. But what you can do is transmit the fear and the anxiety that the main character has for the people he loves and is responsible for. It's become one of the strongest themes running through all of my horror novels. I think it's a lot more terrifying than the fear you feel for your own survival.

So I have a wife and three sons that I care very much about, and if there's any personal experience that comes through my work, it's that constant feeling of looking after them.
GRAHAM MASTERTON

Like everyone, I used to believe in that old theory that by experiencing these horrors vicariously, you are able get them out of your system, and are therefore able to cope with the horrors of reality more efficiently. I don't believe that now. I believe everything you put in your mind stays there. The more crap these kids and young people are putting in their minds, the worse their minds are going to get. Because it doesn't "trickle out" while they're asleep. It's always in there. It's rooted. And one of the proofs is that the only thing that will scare them are things that get worse and worse all the time. *More* horrific. I don't want to blow up an entire field of literature, which would be ridiculous. But we are living in a very violent period of time—

with the drugs, and the street killings, the drive-by shootings . . . New York is like a nightmare, a jungle. Washington D.C. is a total horror. And Los Angeles is apparently now the number one drug center in the country. There's been a general deterioration in society—there's no doubt about it. The horror movies are just a reflection of that.

It's symbiotic: the public wants it, and Hollywood therefore provides it. It's a circle which just goes on and on—they keep making pictures like that knowing they'll succeed, and if some of them don't succeed, they assume it's because they're not horrific enough. So they'll make it even worse.

RICHARD MATHESON

I really do believe in Good and Evil.

I asked a priest once, "Do you think Evil is an actual force?" And he said, "Yes. Undoubtedly—it is an actual force." Of course, being a Catholic, you're brought up with the supernatural. Because if you believe in God, it's as a supernatural being. It's instilled in you. I find it very valuable now as a writer in our genre. Of course, the Catholic Church is supposed to frown on the sort of thing that I do . . . but it's given me so much information and insight on the supernatural!

JAMES HERBERT

I told a story . . . at a convention, a mystery convention. And we were on a panel about fear. There was myself, and there was Robert Morasco—who did *Burnt Offerings*—and there was Janet Jeppson who is Isaac Asimov's wife and who is also a psychiatrist—a clinical psychiatrist. So you know why *she* was there. And that shows where they come from, when they set that panel up!

Somebody in the audience said, "Did anything ever happen to you in your childhood that was really horrible?" And I told a story that I thought would satisfy them. I mean, it isn't anything *I* remember, it's something my mother told me. She said I was out playing one day with this friend of mine. I was about four. I came home, deadly pale, and I'd peed in my pants. And I didn't want to talk. She asked me what happened, but I went upstairs and closed the door and stayed in my room all afternoon. She found out that night that this kid I had been playing with had been run over by a train, okay? I can remember her telling me that they picked up the pieces in a basket. A wicker basket.

I don't remember anything about it; the chances are very good that by that time he had wandered off on his own somewhere, and then I wasn't anywhere around. There's a small chance that maybe I *did* see it happen, maybe the kid chased his ball onto the tracks or something.

So I told this story, and said, "I don't remember it at all," and immediately what Janet Jeppson said was, "And you've been writing about it ever since!!!" The whole audience applauded—because they *want* to believe that you're twisted!

STEPHEN KING

What can I say? The only thing that's ever worked for me was to go where the passion was, to go where the pleasure is, to go where the pain is; to be very intense. Write like mad! Produce. Get the stuff out. I would be lying if I said I wasn't conscious of wanting to write a good story. I'm very conscious of wanting to write an exciting story, a gripping story. And I'm very aware of the fact that that is a commercial element.

With me, the story-telling has always come fairly naturally. Even my earliest work has this terrific narrative drive to it. It's always been a "and then this happened and then that happened" kind of thing. That gives a work a commercial edge. If I was giving advice, I would say don't ignore that.

Remember what Aristotle said two thousand years ago about drama: You have to have plot, character, meaning, and spectacle. So remember that spectacle is important. You had that audience gathered into the arena and you had to show them something that was entertaining. There had to be an element of color, of pageantry, of sensuality. That's how I've always interpreted the term. And in my work, I love to elaborate and amplify the sensuous and dramatic elements. I try to make a very entertaining and spellbinding texture, if I can.

ANNE RICE

I write about people rising to the occasion. Or trying to. One of the conceits of *Off Season* is exactly that: I took two heroines, and I did the *Psycho* "trick" in that I killed the stronger heroine off—in the first reel, so to speak—and you're left with the woman who doesn't believe she has much to go on. And it turns out she has it all. She finds her rage, she finds her courage, she finds the simple will to survive.

And that theme is in everything I've done. I don't think I've ever written anything that didn't have that element. It's almost like a "wish" for me. I wish for my friends to have this gift. For the people that I care about: I wish them always to be able to rise above what they think they can do, to do better.

It's also a wish for myself.

JACK KETCHUM

Richard Matheson tells the story—which was related to me by his son Richard Christian Matheson—that there are people in the world who are going to resent the *mere fact of your existence*. And the fact of the matter is, you don't have to do anything to piss most people off— they're probably going to be pissed off anyway! The mere fact that David J. Schow exists is going to make somebody angry, for whatever reason. You don't get approval about what other people think or say about you. They're going to think it. They're going to say it. You don't get a vote. You can have a reaction to it; you can say, "Hey, wait a minute: that's wrong, that's a mistake." And if it's a really bad mistake, you may wind up taking them to court. (Or plugging them with a 9mm automatic.)

But the fact is you *can't* control every word that's said or printed about you. So the best you can do is offer yourself and your work as a counter-example if the words being said about you are bad.

DAVID J. SCHOW

I know I'm good—without sounding egotistical—because I sell. Consistently. How good I am, I leave that up to the critics. Some people think I'm very good, others think I'm "phony Ray Bradbury"— I know I used to be, when I first started—but I believe I've outgrown that. While Bradbury was one of the writers who influenced me, he wasn't the primary one. That was Nathaniel Hawthorne—and I want to do more like Hawthorne, especially in my shorter work. I want to do a story like "The Black Minister's Veil" or "Young Goodman Browne." God, how I love those stories!

But I really don't know how good I am. All I really care about is that if somebody spends good money on one of my books, reads it through, and gets a good chill now and then, I'm satisfied.

CHARLES L. GRANT

I'm very interested in what turns on the spigot for the dark side that is in all of us, and starts it flowing. A lot of people go through life without ever experiencing that in themselves; yet others get into

situations which cause radical changes in personality. There's apparently an endless supply of situations—as reported in the media. I would be hard-pressed to write anything that would equal the stuff that shows up on television [news] these days. Or to imagine it, really.
JOHN FARRIS

First, before I got married, the protagonist was usually a single guy. When I got married, the protagonist usually had a wife. When we had children, the protagonist usually had a wife and two or more children. The environment for *I Am Legend* was a house in the neighborhood that we lived in; the environment for *A Stir of Echoes* was the house we lived in; the cellar for *The Shrinking Man* was the cellar below the house we were staying in on Long Island. It's much easier to do that than to try and create something out of whole cloth. When I first started *Hell House*, I had difficulty describing the house because I didn't know what to describe; I had nothing in mind. When we went on a family trip to the Hearst Castle, I thought, "This looks just about right." So I got a book there with photographs of all the rooms that I could use to describe in my novel. But certainly, it's always about family to the point where most of my female characters were named "Ruth" in my stories. The children were even named after the names of my children. And the novel *What Dreams May Come* is an *exact* reflection of my family's names, backgrounds—everything.
RICHARD MATHESON

I really did get scathing rejections with *Interview with the Vampire*. And I paid not a whit of attention to them! So you've got to throw that switch in your head that says, "I'm going to succeed!" And you've got to believe in yourself, and you've got to remember that the arts have *always* been tough. There's no point in whining about it. Say if you wanted to become an actor. The first people you would have met would have been sitting around in a cafe saying, "Go home, it's too tough, don't bother!" But it's always been that way in the arts—a bunch of people sitting around telling you that you can't make it. Then others come out of nowhere and go right to the top. What's important is what you've achieved at that moment and if somebody wants it. That's *it*. The arts have been basically the same for two thousand years. You just have to do your best, and make others want your work, and you have to keep looking for the people who want it.

Above all, keep believing in yourself, because nobody can really tell you you're no good.

ANNE RICE

One of my reasons for writing is because my early life was filled with arbitrary tragedies. From the age of ten to the age of twenty, it's just a litany of one catastrophe after another in my family. Beginning with my grandfather's sudden and early death, which really threw the family into a very bad situation. One of my uncles was murdered about a year later. Six months after that, his wife was nearly burned to death, and ended up in the hospital for two years—and she had four kids. My father lost his voice to cancer, and we nearly went bankrupt. Our house burnt down. This all happened at about the same time, and it was like some dark force coming in just striking us, again and again and again.

WHITLEY STRIEBER

When I read horror, I don't read it really to be scared. I read it to be *moved*. So I don't write to scare. If that comes along with it, that's fine. But I write primarily to express emotions, or an idea, or a concept in a certain way. What I try to do primarily is to take the reader into the characters. And if they feel fear, that's fine. If they feel other emotions, that's fine too. But my purpose is not to write a book that is going to "keep you up at night." That's a bonus if that happens. I would prefer that you be moved emotionally the way I try to be moved emotionally when I'm writing it. What excites me is when *I* can really get into a character, and try to feel what he or she is feeling. Then there's the hard part: to get that down on paper. But it's like every day is a new scene, when you're working on a book. Something is going to happen, and your characters are going to do things. It's fun to go along with them.

CHET WILLIAMSON

If [the reader] can find in any of my writings a weirdo with whom it would be pleasant to identify, then I would stand condemned. But I don't believe for example that anybody who has either read *Psycho* or seen the film is inspired to dress up in drag, grab a butcher knife, and head for the nearest shower stall! Because Norman Bateses is *not* presented as a happy human being, or a fulfilled human being. There are no rewards for the Norman Bates of this world in my work. And I don't think there ever will be. There are times when such a person goes unpunished, in the legal sense of the term, but we always know that he or she is a most unhappy person, and much more miserable than any one of the victims.

I don't sit down to try and write a moral homily, but I do believe every writer should have an attitude. When you just present something without a point of view, you're copping-out. As a writer, as a creative individual, you just might as well do a documentary! You've contributed nothing; what you are doing is a fictional report of an atrocity that's meaningless unless you take a position. That position is certainly taken by the press in its reporting. We've yet to see the headlines that say, "Hooray! Twelve More Crimes Committed Today!" or "Wow! What An Axe Murder!" It's a subtle distinction, but it's there.
ROBERT BLOCH

I've been out here since 1955, when I sold *The Shrinking Man* to films, and for all that time—and I've been successful most of that time—I've had very few true creative pleasures. Which is not surprising, of course. If I had had any brains I would have realized that, when you've got that many people working on projects—and the majority of the time most of them are not that talented—that is what's going to happen. Every once in a while there's a rare joining together of really talented forces, and then it turns out great. And then I'm happy. But that happens *so* rarely. I've never knowingly written down to an audience. I've always tried to write the best I can. And I still do. Somehow my numb head has never gotten over the fact that I have to keep doing my best.
RICHARD MATHESON

It just seems to me that you don't ever make a conscious decision to be an artist. You either wake up one day and realize that's what you are or you don't. If that's the case, then nothing can stop you from doing it. And if you're not that kind, then no amount of external rules or enforced discipline is going to force you to it. The motivation is internal, and the rewards are personal.
DENNIS ETCHISON

If my work has had any influence—or if it's had the influence I hope it's had—I can only tell from the feedback I get from my readers.

A) That my novels are literate, and B) they've brought a large measure of believability to the supernatural and to the far-out. This is achieved by technique, by believing in what you're doing, and having respect for the reader.
GRAHAM MASTERTON

Our deep love or interest in horror is a case of being hard-wired, in the sense that it's like putting someone in a front of a Christmas tree and they respond only to a certain kind of ornament.
MATTHEW J. COSTELLO

I think those labels like "dark fantasy" are glossing over what horror really is. I think it's a gut-level kind of writing, an on-the-edge kind of writing.

The problem is not in the writing, or in the writers. The problem is with the publishers. They see horror as primarily a book with some scary elements, and they market it from that narrow perspective. But there's so many different kinds of horror, and so many things going on in horror fiction, that it's very hard to define. But the publishers will try to define it in terms of the marketplace, and will push whatever works. I think it's the writer's responsibility to push the boundaries of what a publisher may feel is "horror fiction." It's the writer who should really get in there and try to do different things within the genre, and push those boundaries. And in that way he'll eventually reeducate the publishers—and the audience—as to what horror fiction is.

I'm not sure myself what horror is. But I know it's *not* just one thing; it's not just *Friday the 13th* or *The Shining* and it's not just *Weaveworld*. It's all those elements—and more.
ROBERT R. McCAMMON

It also goes back to my boyhood—our boyhoods—where everything is sort of awesome.

Like Halloween night, where we were allowed to go around after dark. Onto strange streets. To visit strange houses we'd never been able to go to before. Those are memories that you and I have, that kids today unfortunately don't have. But that sense that the dark itself is scary. And it's not just because there may be people in the dark, it's that total lack of light which in itself is scary. Every time I've ever had a *frisson* of supernatural fear, it's always been in a dark, dark, primordially *dark* place. An old cistern can make me crazy. There's nothing in there—except a sense of the dark being greater than you.

The dark is my church.

JACK KETCHUM

It's kind of touching—[the fans would] like you to be a lot weirder. Of course, you *are* weird. But then, so are *they*!

Boris Karloff was once asked about this...and he said, "Well, one thing that always cheers me, is that even on the brightest, sunniest day, there's always a dark corner... a strange shadow." And he's right; it's always there. It's just part of life, and that's all there is to it.

GAHAN WILSON

If I was going to go crazy, I would have done it by now. But it can get depressing. The novel I just finished, *The Axman Cometh*, which is about an ax murderer, obviously has some depressing aspects. At one point in the book I couldn't proceed. I knew what was coming, I had planned it, it was central to the book—but when I came to it, I just didn't want to do it! I liked the people I needed to get rid of. I had spent a lot of time with these characters, and for the first time since I started writing, I simply could not do something that I had to do. I got to feeling very morbid about this, and I was not fun to be around.

Like an actor getting deeply into a role; you can imagine Laurence Olivier playing Richard III and how much fun he must have been around the house after the show.

JOHN FARRIS

I believe you must first be badly frightened, even if only at an unconscious level, to write believable horror.

J.N. WILLIAMSON

When I read, *I don't care* if it's a "horror novel" or whatever. If it's a good book, with well developed characters that I can become involved with, that's fine. I read *writers*, as opposed to a genre. If I find a writer I like, I'll read his books and I don't care if he writes horror, mystery, Westerns, or all three. When we get into discussing genres, we sometimes tend to get so limited that we forget that there are other kinds of writing out there, including the mainstream.

There's *wonderful* writing in the mainstream. You just have to look for it.

CHET WILLIAMSON

If you have one main book coming out in hardback, and then it's followed the next year in paperback . . . well if I just write those, that leaves me eight months out of the year to sit around and go crazy! So I write the other ones under pseudonyms to keep from going crazy. *I write because I have to write.* I can't go three days without writing something, even a sentence or two. All the books are different, and they're all hard to write. But I just enjoy writing.

CHARLES L. GRANT

Writers are different from other people in one respect: the rewards for our labors are not seen for a long time. Sometimes many years. So we end up learning to operate on faith. "The principle of deferred gratification." Everyone else who has a job receives a paycheck at a regular time; if you're an actor you receive the applause immediately after the performance. A writer will wait months, at the very least, before he receives any kind of feedback. So you learn early on as a writer to go by this principal—of not expecting much in the way of feedback or gratification. So you become toughened, and learn to operate solely out of faith. In that sense, it *is* a spiritual profession.

DENNIS ETCHISON

Because we do this for a living, the basic question most people who interview you keep asking is, "Don't you think this stuff is . . . perverted? Don't you this is sick?" Then I say, "Well, it's no sicker than becoming a politician." But since you have to think abouat that answer, and most people don't bother . . . I remain a pervert.

DAVID J. SCHOW

But my favorite book is *All Heads Turn When The Hunt Goes By*. It's funny how that became my favorite book, because I hated every page of it as I wrote it! It was one of the most difficult books I've ever written. But it stands up pretty well . . . I mean, there's nothing else I've seen or heard that's remotely like it. I had a rough time writing it for a lot of reasons I can't explain. I will say that I ground the last three chapters out the night before I got married, and the publishers were also setting the book up in type as I was going along writing it! And right up until the last night I

didn't know how it would end. I don't mind being in suspense as I go along, but somewhere even *I* like to know where it's going to end! But two years later, I went back and reread it, and I thought, "I wouldn't change a thing."
JOHN FARRIS

One phobia I do avoid is anything happening to children. It's one of the areas that Steve King and I differ on—he would always write about horrible things happening to kids. It's Steve's way of exorcising those fears. And I try to avoid that because it's too meaningful for me, you know? I'd rather run away from it. I've got three daughters, and I find it too painful to write about nasty things happening to kids. I have done it—and I've regretted it afterwards.

I did try once, with a book called *Moon*. The hero had a daughter who was, at that time, the same age as my daughter. And the whole story was leading up to something really terrible that was going to happen to this child. And I couldn't do it! So the dreadful thing that happened, happened to her best friend next door. The reader never got to meet her, and nor did I as a writer—it had to be once removed. It was too horrific. I couldn't get into that terrible emotion of writing about the hero's daughter, because it would have been *my* daughter. And so I just avoided it. Very cowardly—but it was for a reason; it was too much to take.
JAMES HERBERT

. . . In my own short fiction, I've been increasingly able to deal with social issues without necessarily over-stressing my own opinions and values. My opinions are always kept secondary to the plot and to the story, even though my major views are how I define Jerry Williamson to Jerry Williamson. So I've managed to say some things in unpopular areas, such as the topics of abortion and child neglect, without anybody getting violent with me. But if they're reading the story intelligently, it surely must be clear that I'm taking certain stances that may, amongst some people, be highly unpopular. If they understand my ideals and values only subliminally, so much the better. They'll stick, then.
J.N. WILLIAMSON

People who are in the arts like to pontificate that we're doing it out of some deep spiritual commitment . . . *and we are!!* But we are also doing it because, after a while, it's the only thing left that we can do in the world professionally! I never knew it was going to be as hard as it's turned out to be, but after a certain number of years have passed—and you're still working at your profession—you realize that you had better finish what you started and continue onward. The truth of the matter is: what else is left for you? Also, I love the arts. I really feel *committed* to them, almost in a spiritual sense. There's a line which Ray Bradbury has quoted over the years: "There are two honorable professions in the world: doctors, because they heal the body, and artists, because they heal the soul." I just love doing this and, if the truth be told, I wouldn't have it any other way.

DENNIS ETCHISON

I tend to stay away from it all. I don't like horror movies because they scare me half to death! And I don't think you can be a successful horror writer unless you're easily frightened. I have a theory that if nothing frightens you, then you have no way of knowing what's going to frighten other people. Fortunately, I'm a card-carrying coward: *everything* frightens me! I simply transfer all of my own fears on to the paper, and away we go! Consequently, I don't read horror novels, because *they* scare me.

JOHN SAUL

I [have] to figure out—both consciously and unconsciously—what is it about the nature of Evil that really makes it *horrifying*? You start with the basics—putting people in a perfectly ordinary situation and then giving it a twist.

Easier said than done!

JOHN FARRIS

Writing in this genre is comparable to playing the blues. That's really the way I feel about it. The analogy is that there is an incredible amount of richness and variety in what seems to be an extraordinarily limited stock of situations. But it's only limited to the extent that your imagination is limited! You know there's only a certain chord progression, and that's the blues! It goes twelve bars and repeats itself. But—what you can do with that chord progression is staggering.

PETER STRAUB

I liken it to punk music. You remember punk music? There were these so-called musicians whose whole attraction was their sheer, raw energy. That is what carried the music through. Now, the more they played, the better they got. They actually learned how to tune their guitars, for a start. They learned a few more chords. They got better. They got more refined. And of course they faded as time went on. The secret for me has been to maintain that raw energy, *but* learn my craft. Learn to play that instrument without losing that energy.
JAMES HERBERT

...I have interests other than writing. I don't just live to put paper in the typewriter. I like to spend time with my wife and my kids. There's a lot of things I'm interested in that I try to devote time to, because I think you can get very stale as a writer. Those people who just live to write eventually repeat themselves. Besides, what kind of life is that? Go out and get a life!
JOE R. LANSDALE

I, for one, will not play "mind-games" with the people who are good enough to read my work. Why be so pretentious; why try consistently and consciously to create great, subtle "art?" Great art is accidental. Any writer is lucky when it occurs. Entertain and inform and scare them into a few moments of real, reflective thought, and you've done more than most of the writers in any field have achieved.
J.N. WILLIAMSON

...Do I believe in the possibility of evil spirits being influenced by good spirits from another plane, the answer is: probably. I would say I think it's a cinch, though I've never encountered any evil spirits personally. But I do believe everyone has some psychic ability to one degree or another. Through the ages, this has been a common theme in literature as well. There's too much, shall we say, emotional evidence to be ignored.
JOHN FARRIS

It comes down to why you write horror novels, or novels about horror. My philosophy, if I have one, is that the universe is a joke and we are the butt of that joke. And it seems meretricious to me to have a novel about horror with a very happy ending, even with people getting killed along the way. Whereas in life, *the wrong people die.* The good people die young, and the mean ones hang on to the bitter end. And it's also cheating your reader, for them to have ten different characters introduced in the first thirty pages, and be able to pick out which ones are going to die, and which ones are going to survive at the end.

That's cheating. Well, it's not cheating—it's boring! I remember one of the greatest lessons I ever learned was watching a Marco Polo film that came out in the late Fifties or early Sixties. And in it were a Chinese princess and her handmaiden. And the handmaiden died. The princess' handmaiden ALWAYS dies—so that the princess doesn't have to, and she can end up with the hero. You see it all the time, and I *hated* that cheap trick.

MICHAEL McDOWELL

People are usually very disappointed when they get our response, in that most of us aren't out trumpeting the cause in terms of any personal belief in the supernatural. But I guess, in a way, we are. Maybe that's why we write about the unreal—because of this unconscious desire in us to make it real.

THOMAS F. MONTELEONE

It's tough to talk about it, but I think it's valuable, so I'll give it a try. The basic situation was that [my 15-year-old son] Matthew had cancer, and I was convinced he was going to survive it.

To my overwhelming shock, he did not respond to the chemicals he was given. And at a certain point he went into a coma. I sat with him in the intensive care ward, at the University of Iowa hospital. Partially because of the lack of space, the entire family wasn't in there at once—we all took turns. We also took turns because if you spend more than eight hours in an intensive care ward it can really, really have a disastrous psychological effect on you.

So we took shifts. During my eight hours, I was sitting in a corner, looking at Matt while the nurses were doing what was necessary. At one time I counted that the poor kid had three IV poles, with every one of their several hooks filled with various fluids connected to the IV lines. That doesn't take into account the respirator they had down his throat, or the heart monitor which was patched to his chest. Nor the fact that his kidneys had failed and he was on a dialysis machine as well. This poor kid . . . you want to talk about horror: *I was seeing the real thing.*

Stephen King, being the generous and caring man that he is, had periodically been getting in touch with Matt, to try and cheer him up. Sometimes he'd call and sometimes he'd write, and sometimes he'd send a tape because he knew that Matt liked rock 'n' roll as much as Steve does. Sometimes Steve would send a new book. Now, Matt sure wasn't going to get to read the book, which if memory serves, was an advance edition of *The Tommyknockers*.

So I was sitting there. And what I would do periodically is read Stephen's book, and look up at Matt, and see all the tubes and the lights flashing on the monitors, and then I would go back to reading. And we all know the kind of wonderful thing that Steve does with horror: I was reading about people with their hair falling out, and their flesh rotting, and all that. In a certain way, the same sort of thing had happened to Matthew. So I'd read Steve, and look at my son—my poor, bald, puffed-up with steroids son.

Fake horror, such as in Steve's book—and I use the word "fake" with great respect—was somehow acting as an antidote to the real horror around me. It was allowing me to escape to this fantasy world that was believably depicted, but nonetheless *was* fantastic. It was like releasing the pressures that were within me. So, afterwards, I realized that rather than write an entirely different kind of fiction—a very realistic form of fiction, that addressed very real-life concerns—I could, in fact, feel that by writing thrillers or horror that I was performing a very positive function for my readers. That I would be distracting *them* from real horrors with my "fake" horrors.

It was a revelation to me that what we do in this form has such social benefit that I have an obligation to continue doing it. Referring back again to those letters that I received, from people who were asking me to distract them from their problems, I said: "All right—let's get back to work." I guess I have to be very thankful to Stephen for all kinds of reasons, not only for his generosity to my son, but also just for the example that he provided.

DAVID MORRELL

Speaking as a devout agnostic, I do think that the spiritual side of horror fiction is not explored enough. I think there is a market for it, a desire for it by the readers, and if the writer can touch on that issue, he can have a good career. He can say something, and have a good career. There is a spiritual side to all of us, and I don't necessarily mean a soul. But rather a yearning within human beings for transcendence. For a hint that it all doesn't end here; that there is something beyond

this life, our physical bodies. And if you can address that in your fiction, then you will speak to a lot of people, and a lot of people will listen.
F. PAUL WILSON

I would say there is definitely some kind of psychological or emotional engine that propels one to do this. Clearly. I think of that when I read Stephen King, and he writes some particularly vicious action scene, and I think, "Wow! The engine that drives his imagination is one that runs down that track." But I could say that about Edgar Allan Poe, or H.P. Lovecraft. I could say that Franz Kafka's engine of imagination was really pretty grim! I don't know if I would have ever imagined a story where I woke up one morning and turned into a bug. But in making movies, I think you have to be attracted to the visualization of terror. You have to repeat to yourself a little litany that goes something like this: "The strongest emotion is fear. The oldest emotion is fear. We all have it, and it is a very deep pool inside every human on the planet." So there are some of us who dive into that pool because we are both repelled and attracted by it. But I think a lot of directors who make horror films sleep pretty well at night, because they're able to express through their movies very hateful and vengeful feelings. We're kind of engaged in this ongoing, life therapy.... George Romero is one of the nicest, straightest, most innocent and fun-loving people I know of. Very relaxed, very conservative! He's like a be-bop hipster from the Fifties.
JOHN CARPENTER

What I have been looking for, and what I'm always looking for, is an edge to throw myself over. Too far ... it's the only place to go! To seek out what seems to be the most extreme elements, and then try and stretch myself to the point where I can relate with it creatively— that's what keeps me going.
ALAN MOORE

There are many reasons why I don't want the label ["horror writer"]. I don't want to be limited as to what I can write; I want to be able to write what I want.

For example, when I signed a recent three-book deal with Putnam, the most appealing clause in the contract was that they wouldn't know anything about the contents of the books, not even the titles, until the delivery of the manuscripts. That's the only way I want to write. I write what I want to read, what appeals to me, and what excites me at the moment. A second reason is that I don't exactly like a lot of what usually carries the Horror label. Any time there's a "boom" in the genre, you find yourself mixed in with a lot of writers who are grabbing what's popular at the moment, and who are writing it because there's a market for it, not out of true passion. So you end up being tarred with that same brush.

DEAN KOONTZ

I take it pretty seriously. I don't mind being called a horror writer. Dean Koontz, I know, has his problems with being known as one. And I like to *read* horror—always have. I can't possibly enjoy writing something I don't enjoy reading, otherwise I would be a very rich and famous writer of Romances by now.

GARY BRANDNER

I guess in an ideal world I would object to being called a horror writer. But I think the term has taken on connotations that, in many cases, don't really fit what I or a lot of other writers are doing. I think both readers and writers are pretty much forced to use a vocabulary that's created to serve the needs of the publishers and marketing people. The label "horror writer" is pushed on us by people who put books on shelves, or on lists, rather than chosen by the writers themselves.

JOSEPH A. CITRO

Let's deal with the craft of storytelling. I think the whole purpose to telling a story is to take the audience on a journey which they otherwise wouldn't get to take. It's one of the reasons why I've never been deeply interested in what we'll loosely call "naturalistic fiction." Were I to write the male menopause novel—when I reach that age—I would presumably be addressing it to only those people who were actually having a male menopause. Which does not seem to me to be a hugely interesting process.

Let's go only where *imagination* can take us! Some of those places are going to be very dark and dangerous, and yes, they're going to be "over the edge of the map," if you like. They are going to be the places where we can confront the forbidden. Some of them are also going to be "dreamscapes" where we can feel reassured, and where we feel as though we have a glimpse of comprehension rather than of panic. I am as interested in those areas as I ever have been; I'm interested in ecstasy *and* terror. I'm particularly interested in the place where one becomes the other. Those two extremes are the twin beacons out there, and I'm most excited when I actually find that I've reached one.

Then I want to reach the other.

CLIVE BARKER

I would also say: *never give up.* I once had a story rejected 72 times; it took me six and a half years to sell it. But I *did.* It's like going to a party where there are 60 people. You can't expect to please all of them. But if you can just meet the right one, then you can forget the 59 others you never connected with.

DENNIS ETCHISON

People expect us to look like Christopher Lee and wear a black cape, don't they?

JAMES HERBERT

Generally speaking, I think good horror fiction has been the fiction of the confessional. *Books of Blood* was very *much* about what was going on inside me at the time. I think that in order to convince readers that these extraordinary events are valid and real, you *have* to be writing from deep places in your psyche. You can't construct these things casually or in a detached fashion. They are passions that are rooted in your deepest feelings; in my case, they always have been.

CLIVE BARKER

Getting older, and being a parent and having kids (and becoming sort of the person in the cave who protects everybody, and assures them there are no bears in here), I find the world a less scary place on a supernatural plane, and a more scary place on a realistic plane. Which is probably why my more recent work has been more mainstream suspense, because that to me is a believable fear. It's hard to make myself believe any more that Cthulhu is plotting to make that big leap from across the universe and plop in my backyard! Vampires are also a hard sell. Stephen King made it work in *'Salem's Lot*, but I think the last thing I'm prepared to be nervous about is someone's going to suck my blood—as opposed to steal my wallet.

But this is a natural transition. You reach a point in your life where you let go of a lot of things from your youth, and one of the things you let go of as you get older is that almost childish belief in supernatural fears. Unless your goal as a writer is to stay in touch with that "inner child" and your inner child [purposely chooses to] remember what that's like.
MATTHEW J. COSTELLO

I use a *tremendous* amount of autobiographical material, and I use a lot of my own fears. I use a lot of the fears of other people, that they've told me. But usually if I can't put something of myself into the stories, I can't write them. Which is not the same thing as saying the stories represent all my beliefs, but they are boiled down from my subconscious. Mainly it's autobiographical elements from personal attitudes and beliefs or experiences.
JOE R. LANSDALE

The Sandman is an entertainment. It's a delightful entertainment, even though I've had to work harder and longer and it's given me more headaches than anything else I've had to do. But I think it's something to do with choosing your targets, who your audience is. And yes, my audience is me. That is, at the end of the day, the person I'm writing to please most is myself.
NEIL GAIMAN

It works best if I can scare myself. When I was writing *Cameron's Closet*, I used the closet right across from my office room here as a model. And I kept looking over there when I was writing the scarier parts, and would hear these strange noises from in there! And if I can do *that* to myself, then I figure the writing is going well.
. . . When I'm really involved in a story, then I really believe in the subject while I'm writing. If I'm writing about werewolves, then I believe at the time in werewolves. I would have to say I can't absolutely deny the possibility of anything.
GARY BRANDNER

Whatever is wrong that makes me this way—I have a fairly solid commitment to it. In *Living In Fear*, I think I called it partially a "left-handed religious impulse;" that there is some fascination with mortality and death which is a major issue—unless either by being deeply religious or an atheist one knows precisely what is going to

happen after death—that is a topic worthy of concern. I don't claim to be giving any pat answers, but there is a fascination that makes me want to speculate on it. This is part of what keeps me going. And just to realize it's possible to "knock somebody's socks off" with stories about this subject inspires me. I don't know if it's the kind of inspiration that most people would be glad to have, but I assume a certain number of people will relate to what I'm saying.
LES DANIELS

I firmly believe [we] are born this way. The trouble with the genre at the moment is that there *are* too many horror writers who are manufactured; not natural horror writers. It's a booming industry, it's an exciting industry, and a lot of these guys don't work by instinct, they work by process, if you like. They've read a lot of good horror over the years, and a lot of *bad* horror over the years, and they emulate it. It doesn't come from deep within. With me, there must be some twisted side of my nature that just *loves* horror. And I think that's true of the best of us, it really is. There's something within us that is, I think, a bit warped, and you're born with that. It's not manufactured.
JAMES HERBERT

It's easy to blame others when you have bad luck, but when you stop and analyze what's happened to you, you may realize that it was just as much your fault as the rest of the world's. So that only makes you resolve to not make those mistakes again, and to try a little harder. J.G. Ballard has spoken of life as a search for psychological closure, and Philip K. Dick suggested that we may be unconsciously seeking a kind of stasis or dead-end, a corner into which we've painted ourselves and from which there is finally no escape.

This is the most chilling concept I have ever encountered—that our best efforts at growth, self-help, health and progress may in fact be designed, albeit unconsciously, to achieve quite the opposite: to bring about our own entrapment and defeat. In other words, that what we think we are doing and what we are *actually* doing may be diametrically opposed; that the human animal may be programmed for self-defeat on a level that is not accessible to consciousness or mutable by will. Not just that the unconscious may throw up barriers and obstacles, out of some deep-seated conviction that we do not deserve to win, but that the unconscious may ultimately *refuse to allow* our success because it is pre-programmed toward a different goal or purpose that we may never know and might not be able to comprehend.

I pray to God that this is not true, but you never know.
DENNIS ETCHISON

I used to think you had to have a very keen perception of what people are afraid of. But that really doesn't work, because subjectively we're all afraid of different things. Our fears are all hard-wired into us when we're born, or they're things we pick up at a very early age that really, really bother us on some very basic level. Most of us can't articulate these fears. We just don't know why some people are afraid of insects, some people are afraid of snakes—while some people aren't afraid of either.

But a horror writer has to have an unconscious sense or knowledge of what's going to be a universal "trigger." I don't know if you can teach it. If it works well in your writing, then you've got it. It's an unconscious sense. Because there's a psychological response to fear, and a biological response. But a good writer can accomplish both those responses in the reader. I remember when Stephen King wrote about some character's "testicles shriveling up." And I thought, "My God, that really does happen!"

It's just that sense of *what is the right response* during that encounter with fear. The *true* response. And I think that, if as a writer you have that ability to capture that true response all of us feel, you have a unique talent. A talent which doesn't come along that often.
THOMAS F. MONTELEONE

One of the things that psychiatry—the Freudian brand—is supposed to do is to allow you to open up lines of communication from your subconscious to the outside, where you can finally externalize it to the world. So, on the one hand, we say that psychiatry allows us to talk about our innermost fears, and that's wonderful, it helps you to get "normal." But if you do what I do, you *must* be "weird" because those channels are *open*. If they were closed, people would say you're normal, because you *can't* talk about your fears. You're all fucked up! Situation normal: all fucked up.
STEPHEN KING

My personal fears wouldn't really make for interesting fiction. I think it goes deeper than that, from people like Stephen King and

Peter Straub and me to everybody else in the field right down to the first time novelist; they're not doing this to just make a buck. They're really working on something that is intimately involved in their psyche—and this is going on 29 or 30 books for me—and *I'm* still trying to work it out, whatever "it" is. I don't know if I'm any closer to the end or not. I write a great deal of poetry. And I find that I can say something concisely in a poem that, for me, is a more concrete way of getting down on paper whatever it is that's in the deep-most part of your psyche. There are things that I would never put down in a novel, that I can put into a poem—and hope nobody ever reads it.

JOHN FARRIS

Any horror movie or book—even a good one—if you stop and think about the majority of 'em, the idea's *stupid*. Unless you really believe in vampires and witches and werewolves. Of course horror has moved in considerably different directions from that, which I believe it has to—we've outgrown it for the most part. Which is not to say people shouldn't write about these supernatural creatures—I'm not saying I wouldn't do it. But in modern times, they become more representative of modern themes, rather than simply being vampires and witches and werewolves. They may have had some psychological representation in the past, but they must have even more now if they're to be used effectively. They represent today's society.

I hadn't thought about it before, but it's almost Lovecraftian in that I often deal with the breakdown of what you think are the expected rules of existence. In a sense, I guess that's what H.P. Lovecraft was doing with his Cthulhu mythos, except he had them explained as aliens or entities.

JOE R. LANSDALE

I like to think that what I do is of some use, but frankly I'm dubious. As I've said on previous occasions, one of the greatest flourishings of humor and satire of all time in the arts was in Germany during the rise of Hitler and that whole period. A lot of that satire was directed at Adolf himself. But it didn't do a damn thing to stop him. When push came to shove, he just said, "Kill them." And that was that. It didn't even slow him down. But I figure what the hell—full speed ahead. Sometimes it works. Humor is great at saying the emperor has no clothes. So maybe.

GAHAN WILSON

For all the violence in my books, I think they're basically fairly optimistic about the human potential: "We may get slaughtered, murdered, have our ears cut off... but then we can still go beat the bad guys!"
JACK KETCHUM

I just really deal with whatever obsesses me at the moment. As a writer, I feel like I'm about five different people, and only one of them writes the vampire novels. Also, frankly, in the beginning, I was afraid of being typecast as a "horror writer." ... I'm not in the least bit afraid now. That was before I understood that it didn't really matter; that the horror fans were easily the most intelligent and perceptive fans the books could have. I mean, you can do *anything* in that genre. You can write a great, great, great novel in the horror genre. There's nothing in it that forces you to write less well, or to create shallow characters. I'd be very happy now if I were to write nothing but occult novels under the name Anne Rice.
ANNE RICE

I *have* to be frightened by what I'm doing. There has to be at least one moment—hopefully it's underlying through the whole experience—when I shut off that word processor at the end of the day, and the house is dark and quiet, and there is a true feeling of *fear* in me. Hopefully, I've transmitted it to the reader as well. That effect, I think, is very important. It's like when you're writing a sexual story: there should be a strong feeling of eroticism. When you're writing an adventure story, you want to be thrilled by it and want to know what will happen next.

So I think it's very, very important for a horror writer to be frightened by his own work.
GRAHAM MASTERTON

Writing about vampires doesn't make me a bloodsucker; writing about homicidal maniacs doesn't mean I'm a maniacal murderer myself. Intellectual curiosity is a far cry from obsession.
ROBERT BLOCH

Guys like me, we were duds in high school. Writing has always been *it* for me. I was just sort of this nerdy kid. I didn't get beat up too much because I was big, played a little football and stuff like that. So mostly I just got this, "King—he's weird. Big glasses. Reads a lot. Big teeth." I've

thought about stopping—sometimes it seems to me I could save my life by stopping. Because I'm really compulsive about it. I drive that baby. . . .
STEPHEN KING

I find that I entertain myself: at three o'clock in the morning, I'm pounding away on the typewriter and having a hell of a time. So I keep doing it.
LES DANIELS

Just the fact that I've been able to scare people doesn't make me a great guy. I've entertained them, that's about all you can say.
RICHARD MATHESON

A theme that runs throughout most of my dark fiction: the loss of mental control and what results from this twisted emotional condition. Most of my characters walk a tightrope between sanity and insanity, and I find the breakdown of the human mind to be an endlessly fascinating subject.
WILLIAM F. NOLAN

I was raised with a very strict religious background, and that created a lot of inherent rage, and in a way I just stumbled onto this way of expressing myself. Another thing is when you become very good at something that is as extraordinary as horror films (and I use that word as a neutral term), it's extraordinary in the sense that this is not something most people express an affinity with. Most people shy away from dealing with emotions such as rage, extreme anger, and other bizarre and irrational behavior. Most adults are uneasy with dealing with any of that, and don't actively explore it artistically. I went through a period in my career when anyone that I met was astonished to see that I was the person making these kind of films. I've gotten out more in recent years and met other directors working in this genre, and they all tell similar stories. People react to Clive Barker in the same way. Sam Raimi is like that—they tend to be fun-loving people. Very upbeat, very "normal" people. Yet the audience, and many of the critics, still assume we must be very strange and unhappy people.
WES CRAVEN

To return to the term "dark suspense," the abnormal psyche is an endless source of material, of interesting stories. I dislike writing the same book over and over again. I prize humor in writing, concentrated plots, rich characters, good versus evil; I like a happy ending. I like stories which I can use as a vehicle to show off; I mean that in a good sense, to show off what I can do. And I can do a hell of a lot. This type of fiction gives me the opportunity to take chances.

JOHN FARRIS

My horror fiction is a catalog of my fears.

I was interviewed in England once, and the interviewer said, "In almost all your stories, the biggest fear seems to be a loss of control, or a loss of self." And he got right to the heart of it: that, to me, is the ultimate fear. To lose control over what you are. Over who you are. Or what you want to be. To wind up being less of a person than you wish to be, than you'd always hoped you'd be; than you thought you were. ... It's there in *The Keep*. It's there in *Sibs* ... so many of my books!

I've never really articulated that fear to myself. But it's there. In the books.

F. PAUL WILSON

Most writers cannot successfully get past that "membrane" which separates childhood from adulthood. Unless we get out our pocket knives, cut a hole in it, and let those childhood fears pass through. I think that's what a lot of horror and dark suspense horrors have done—they've really invited those early fears to come along and stick around, so they can now draw on them creatively.

THOMAS F. MONTELEONE

I'm not really sure that I chose to write "horror fiction." I was always attracted to certain tales in the area of Vermont where I grew up: folktales and legends that had been around a long time. And I thought, "Maybe there's a market for these stories." Even if there wasn't a market, I didn't want to see the stories vanish altogether—so I wrote them down. The horrific elements in these folktales were so strong that I knew I would be dealing with horror, maybe not as a type of literature, but in the sense of great *fear*. The characters in my books would ultimately be confronting something tremendously scary.

JOSEPH A. CITRO

Every kid got this: "Monsters are bad for you; they'll warp your mind ... " But kids don't have the option then of turning around and saying, "What are you *talking* about?" If the people who are criticizing the genre ever had to explain themselves, their argument would fall to pieces with terrifying speed. Because what do they present as an alternative? The same shit you got in high school, when they look at you during those career courses and say, "You have to give yourself some basis for having a good and productive *job*. So you can be an upstanding citizen, a wonderful father, and a good provider. And most of all, a good *consumer* when you grow up." To me, the idea of locking yourself in that box from high school on, is scarier than anything I could write.

DAVID J. SCHOW

Unless I get really fired up by an idea, I'm just terribly lazy . . . ! I can while away the day very easily. I'll take a walk in the park. Or watch "Court TV." (I watched every day of the Simpson trial because I wasn't working on anything. Though I told myself, maybe I'll use this trial someday in a novel to justify it.) When I do get fired up, I'm a workaholic. But it's only during that period for that one particular work. Then I tell myself I'm letting "the well" fill up again—though it does feel an awful lot like loafing. But I do go to the desk everyday. I feel guilty if I don't at least explore the possibility of actually working.

IRA LEVIN

The whole essence of being an effective "horror person" is to be able to communicate effectively to the reader—or viewer—the knowledge—sure and certain—that we are mortal, and could drop dead at any moment. That we are walking on thin ice—always—twenty four hours a day.

Both of these insights tend to give to these personalities two steady moods. One is of gentleness. I've noticed over the years that horror people—more than science fiction writers, more than mystery writers, more than any other genre of writers I know—are kindly. Some of them are bastards, sure, but most of them are quite kindly and sweet. You'll see that when fans come up to them—they tend to be especially nice to the fans. Horror people are just nice people; they really are! I think the reason why is because they know the fragility of their fans because they already know the fragility of themselves as human beings.

GAHAN WILSON

CHAPTER NINE

Shocking Advice

I think all of us start in darkness.

I try to encourage young writers to face up to their hostilities and murderousness. A lot of us were raised incorrectly, and we're supposed to be ashamed of our feelings, and ashamed of our destructiveness. We *should* be, if we take a direct object and go out and destroy it. Because we don't want that for ourselves we have to find ways of doing these things indirectly. And so I try to say, "Look: pin the shadows to the wall first! Get rid of the dinosaurs and tyranosauri—and all those other monsters and ghosts and skeletons in your subconscious. Open Pandora's Box! Let out the horrors!"

Those are the first truths you know.

RAY BRADBURY

There really must be a love of just working the language. A delight in making sentences. There's a wonderful character in this Philip Roth novel that I enjoyed very much, *The Ghost Writer*, who's an old writer. He says, "I get up in the morning and I write a sentence. And then I turn the sentence around." You really have to like doing that! That's essential—that's the nuts and bolts. You really have to get a deep joy out of writing itself. And out of other people's writing, too.

PETER STRAUB

Even Shakespeare would not have written a play unless it was exciting and full of surprises. So don't think that the commercial and intellectual are at odds with one another. They're not. You can write

127

a great novel and have it be really suspenseful and have a lot of spectacle to it. Yet it can still have all the philosophy and deep meaning that your soul needs to make your writing worthwhile.
ANNE RICE

Writing is a *job*. It is plain hard work. Anyone who's gone to college and written term papers knows what I mean. Just think of doing it every day, five days a week. Or three days one week and four another—whatever schedule suits you. Just as long as you do have a schedule, and even if you have a job on the side—which most people must have when they're beginning to write seriously. I run every morning before I go to work. I *hate* running. But I do it because it's beneficial, and I know other good things are going to come because of it. When you start out cold, saying to yourself "I can't do this today," the first couple of laps are murder. Then you get yourself into a groove, and find that the experience becomes pretty mechanical, if not enjoyable. It's that way when you sit down to write something as long and difficult as a novel. Doesn't matter whether you can do it better in the morning or better at night; you have to establish a regular time to write. It may be a paragraph or a page, who knows? But if you stay with it, the pages pile up, and you'll write a book.
JOHN FARRIS

I was in a Waldenbooks store the other day, and I ran into an acquaintance of mine who used to be a doctor. She decided to quit the profession to pursue a full-time career as a science fiction writer. I said to her, "What are you working on these days?" She replied, "A science fiction novel, set in the future, which has to do with medicine." I said, "Well, let me make a suggestion. There are the bestsellers over there—do you find any science fiction among them?" (And I didn't mean an Asimov or a Clarke or a *Star Trek*, all of which are special cases.) She didn't of course, because science fiction novels don't often appear on the list, and we notice it when they do because we aren't *expecting them to*. So what I said to her was, "For heaven's sake, don't tell your editor or your agent that you're writing a science fiction novel, set in the future, about medicine. Tell them you're working on a *futuristic medical thriller*." Her eyes lit up, and she began to understand the logic that I was using. We avoided the "science fiction" label. "Futuristic medical thriller" had such a good sound to it, hell, I was ready to try one! My point is that often it's a question of marketing. There are writers in the horror field whom I have *immense* regard for. But they have never been able to break through; to get on the best-seller lists. They may be widely respected within the genre, but they don't have the broader base of readers outside their field.

It may be that some people working within the horror form are doing their careers harm by thinking too "small," for lack of a better word. There was a panel of very experienced editors at a recent Horror Writers of America conference talking about what makes for a break-through book. They were saying it's not so much the field that you're working in, it's the "canvas." (I hate using that overworked word, but it's one we all understand.) The scope and the breadth of the book. Most horror novels tend to be short, they tend to be inbred—they rely on the ideas and concepts of others who have gone before them. Of course, a horror writer ought to be aware of the history of the genre. But to sell a lot of copies, a horror writer also has to find a large idea and head toward uncharted territory, announcing, in effect, that this book is *different* from other horror fiction.

Easy to say. Very, very difficult to do.

DAVID MORRELL

I spoke with Richard Matheson recently, and he said, "When I was back in college, we were taught that there were three kinds of stories: pulp, slick, and literary. But they were wrong. There are two kinds of stories: good and bad." I don't consider myself a "horror writer." I am just a writer of popular fiction who likes to work in every genre but romance. The best kind of fiction is the result of the writer giving us his own feelings about things.

I recently re-read Matheson's *Ride The Nightmare*, a wonderful 1958 suspense novel, and in the course of all the non-stop action, I was able to hear Matheson imparting his view of marriage, being a parent, and being a man too timid to extricate himself from terrible trouble—and losing his self-respect (maybe even his manhood) in the process. Now, I'm not talking about Matheson giving us any direct addresses or writing obtrusive mini-essays on the themes of the novel. But by the time you finish the book, you know a lot more about Richard than when you started it. It's all there—in the action, attitudes, and plot turns of the book. (John D. MacDonald also had a similar ability, especially in his paperback originals of the Fifties.) Without such grace notes, *Ride The Nightmare* would have been just another slick but empty paperback. Matheson made it into a master-piece and it reads as well today as it first did in 1958.

Good novels are a lot more than plot and literary special effects.

ED GORMAN

But what the other new writers have done—King especially—is work out a form for the horror novel that has qualities which allow it to get into the mainstream, and bestseller, class. A lot of strong, realistic treatments. Take *The Shining* for example. Even without the Overlook Hotel, the main character has enough problems to make him fascinating enough to write a book about. And when you put in the supernatural, why it's only an addition to all his personal prob-lems! But I'd say King was vital in making the basic story so emotion-ally strong—strong enough to stand even without the horror element—that when you add in the horror element too, why, you have the makings of a good mainstream novel.

And a bestseller.

FRITZ LEIBER

If you're a horror writer, then you want to be able to jolt or scare. It's different from suspense because it's like peaks of electricity. And they should come—you should be able to do them—so that they come in the right places. You have to make sure they have the right rhythm of low peaks, middle peaks, and high peaks. I suppose there are equivalent ones, but they have to be layered in, and they have to be invisible in the narrative. That is, you have to have not only suspense, and not only characterization, and not only follow through on plot, but you have to have these "jolts." And that's something quite techni-cal; I don't know if you can learn it.

MICHAEL McDOWELL

You have to remember that the hero of the book is usually the author's alter-ego, so therefore your hero is thinking thoughts that you, the writer, would think. You can't avoid that, and [so] your worst sort of phobias and fears come out.

JAMES HERBERT

I've never really written for any market. I didn't really decide to write "horror fiction," but that's the way my work is marketed. "Joseph Citro does for Vermont what Stephen King does for Maine" is the publisher's idea of marketing. I've always been afflicted with a very personal vision. And that personal vision is the one I afflict on the reader. If they want to see Vermont through my eyes, to take an unconventional look, that's a good reason to read my work. Another reason is that so much of the gothic and horror tradition in this country comes from New England. The settlers who first came here were Europeans, who were all raised on demonology and a fire and brimstone kind of religion. Imagine them snowbound in their remote farmhouses on dark New England nights. Imagine thick woods and unfamiliar land. Imagine the savages and the beasts they believed were surrounding them. Is it any wonder their minds turned to dark thoughts? So in a sense, writing about the myths and legends of New England is a return to basics. Perhaps it helps that I am a native New Englander, and have lived here all my life, so far.

JOSEPH A. CITRO

There are really two aspects, and they're contradictory. One is the enormous *fun*, and anybody who is a writer does it because that's what he likes to do. You enjoy it. But there is also the unutterable *tedium* of it, and I don't think most people can take it. When people say "Gee, I wish could do what you do...." I wouldn't wish it on anyone—because you spend most of your life alone in a room.

PETER STRAUB

Never, never, never, as long as you live, revise a manuscript on the basis of a rejection letter. Never! Only revise that manuscript when you get the acceptance letter. Nine out of ten times, somebody who rejects a manuscript doesn't really know why they don't like it, and they're just saying something to you to try and get their feelings down—and it's probably stupid. Because if you could talk to them for twenty minutes, you would know they didn't read your book carefully, and that they weren't right audience for it anyway. It's one of the most heartbreaking things in our profession, the writer who takes a whole manuscript and starts revising it because some idiot editor says "I'd like your novel better if everybody in it was an Indian." Or whatever. So the writer does it, and a year later, the editor sends it back saying, "I don't like it any better than I did before." *Don't ever fall into that trap*. Remember, these are people who are buying or rejecting on the most whimsical basis, and it's nothing worth listening to.

ANNE RICE

I still believe that anyone who says they actually enjoy the process of writing is not working hard enough at it.
JOHN SAUL

I don't think you should be petulant of what you do. If you take on a project, you should find some way of doing it with a good heart. I find it contemptible when people slough something off, or when people think a project isn't worth their best effort on it. It makes me furious: "Oh, what are people going to think of me if I throw myself into this project, body and soul?" You know? "People should think I'm saving myself for something better." I'm appalled by that attitude. I love working in horror—because I find it very difficult to do. I think it's very difficult to find new jolts—to find new ways of twisting the knife. And new places to stick the knife.
MICHAEL McDOWELL

Write what you feel. Never write "to market." (I have, and have always regretted it.) What hurts you, what makes you angry, what you feel gives dignity and purpose to your life. And this is true no matter what you're writing—short stories, novels or screenplays. Write every day if possible. Set a number of pages for yourself—one or two, if you're working part-time; four to six if you're writing full-time. This is what works for me but it may not work for you. The important thing is to discipline yourself enough to put your butt in that chair day in and day out.

As for advice on writing stories versus novels—I always find a model for what I'm writing. For instance, the other day I was writing a story that was about a teenager who suddenly finds himself in terrible trouble. I hauled out my Ed McBain story collections and found a couple with the sort of structure I had in mind. McBain wrote some very good juvenile delinquent stories back in the Fifties and Sixties. Reading three of his stories helped me enormously. They were like taking vitamins. I sat down and got to work. I do the same thing with novels and screenplays, read one or two that might help me with the project at hand. Yours won't end up even remotely like your model but finding the model will help—or maybe not. As Somerset Maugham said in 1903, "There are three rules for writing the novel. Unfortunately, nobody can remember what they are."

Each writer has to figure out what works best for him or her. You may find everything I do silly, impractical, and unnecessary. Fine.

Find your own method. That's what it's all about. The important thing is to apply butt to chair every day and then you and your own idiosyncrasies take it from there.

ED GORMAN

As far as someone setting out to become a genre writer, I think many people *do* begin their careers by thinking, "Oh, I'm going to write mysteries." "I'm going to write science fiction." Or "I'm going to write horror." And hopefully the reason they want to write in those fields is because that's the kind of book they're truly interested in; they're not just getting on some kind of bandwagon. I think the main reason a writer should dwell in a genre is because it *obsesses* them. If you feel you're basically a horror writer, then go for it! Don't decide, "Well, the real money is in courtroom dramas—I'll write a John Grisham type courtroom novel." Don't do it! Follow your own inclinations instead.

RICHARD LAYMON

When you mail out a manuscript, you are not turning in a paper for a grade. You can mail out a perfectly wonderful and publishable novel and have it rejected ten times. And the reason it's rejected is because you hit ten different people who for various reasons don't want to work with this idea. You have to keep going. You have to never interpret rejection from New York publishers as a failing grade.

They are not failing grades. They mean almost nothing.

ANNE RICE

The first novel I ever wrote didn't sell. But it got some nice feedback. Some editors actually sent back personal notes, and new writers should realize that's your first leg up in the business: when you get a rejection and someone puts a personal comment on it. That's your first success, when you get that rejection with some encouraging information attached to it.

I actually came to writing short stories after I sold my first novel, and I sold my first novel after I spent some time working in the field of journalism.

But if I was starting out today, probably the way to go about it would be with the small press. Learn to find your own voice through short stories, because at the same time you're then making contact with editors. And you're starting to get your name out there, even on a small scale, so that people in the business know you. So when the time comes to try to pitch a proposal for a novel, you will have already gained some experience in the field you want to work in.

And you'll know who the editors are, and you may already have achieved some recognition in that, if they're reading some of the same magazines you're appearing in, they'll know who *you* are. Already they're more favorably disposed to looking at your work as a professional. Whereas just coming in off of the street, I think it would be a lot harder.

MATTHEW J. COSTELLO

I once gave a speech at a writer's conference on why I hate genres. Do everything you can to destroy genres. *A good story is a good story.* If you tell a love story, and you set it on Mars, then it's a science fiction story. You tell it set in the old West, and it becomes a Western. You tell it in the midst of a detective story, and it's a detective story. And so on and so forth. This idea that there's this "genre" that exists like a steel coffin, and you've got to jump inside it to write your story.... In many cases, it's not that these writers, including Robert Bloch and myself, have not attempted other fields. It's just that there's not a welcome mat in these other fields and they've got to *batter* their way into it if they're going to do it. And even if they do it, the long-time readers are going to say, "Aww, gee, why don't you do the old stuff?"

RICHARD MATHESON

Good writing in itself is a pleasure, and it can seduce you into the story. I'm not very concerned with style or anything like that, but I *am* concerned with the balance. Language should have a balance, and it should be a balance the reader can feel and get into, and feel a sort of rhythm to the language as it moves along. The language should be able to carry you into the story. And that's *it*. Because if the reader is seduced into the story, then it carries him away.

STEPHEN KING

One way which I can productively use this brimming over of ideas is to get into different fields—like comic books. I've also been writing more short stories lately for various anthologies. It's a different way of expressing the same ideas which may eventually make novels, but which will certainly help develop the terror—and develop my own techniques. You never stop learning; you never stop expanding your techniques and ideas.

I *do* have a lot of ideas, so this in some ways is the problem. But it's also the joy of imagining these other realities and possibilities and other lives. Imagining new fears, exploring various frights. Being able to convey this to other people is a *joy*. My biggest axe to grind is with publishers who fail to see the author-editor-publisher-distributor-reader as one direct link. There are so many good books published today (and some of mine are included amongst those) that are badly published. They just don't reach the public that they ought to.

Unfortunately, too many writers today are writing for the publisher, and not for the reader.

GRAHAM MASTERTON

"Serious Advice For Young Writers Who Want To Break Into The Field?" The first thing they have to do is *read*. Not just the horror field; that's the worst thing they can do. They have to read *everything* they can get their hands on. They've got to read Dickens, and Twain and Shakespeare. And poetry. And they've got to read the contemporary masters. Before they can write, they've got to learn good writing. They have to learn what makes a good story, and what makes a good novel, first. *Read*! Watch less television! Exercise the imagination! Learn to use the goddamn language. Stay away from manuals of style and "creative writing" classes—they don't do a goddamn thing for you. I get a lot of submissions [when editing an anthology] after a hit movie comes out—and there'll be tons of stories that are *almost* the same as the movie. But those people can't write—and they never will. Not without an imagination. And you have to know the rules before you can break the rules. Somebody who wants to write something different can't do it any differently until they know how it's done right. Then they can twist and turn and learn to develop their own style and voice.

CHARLES L. GRANT

For anyone who wants to be a writer, I simply say "to thine own self be true." The major gift that anyone has to give is not a technical gift, but the gift of their own personal vision. We all know authors who are not great stylists, but whose vision is compulsive reading. And we also know great prose stylists who we fall asleep in front of. I've always told young writers to find that part of yourself that is uniquely you—find those visions which everyone else has said you should have nothing to do with, that forbidden part, and write them.

Tell the world about the dark stuff, and do it without embarrassment.

CLIVE BARKER

There may be other ways [to generate fresh ideas], but I only know one. You have to read enormous amounts of material of all kinds; you have to be constantly feeding the subconscious, giving it material from which it can devise story ideas. First you must read nonfiction of all kinds, not just in areas that already interest you, but in a wide range of subjects. I regularly read books and magazines about the latest developments in genetics, physics, medical technology, forensic medicine, police technology and procedure, and much more. I read a daily newspaper, three Sunday newspapers, and scores of magazines every month. I never take notes, and I never consciously look for story ideas; it's a much subtler process than that. You pour the information into the subconscious, dump it all in like meat and vegetables into a stew pot, then let it cook until the ideas boil to the surface. They *will* boil up, I guarantee, and they'll be far better than the ones you arrive at by conscious manipulation of story elements, better because they're not forced. Then you have to read fiction, too, lots of it, and not only in one or two genres. I read mysteries, suspense, science fiction, horror, Westerns, mainstream, everything. The more you read, the more you become aware of the techniques that are special to every genre, and the more you begin to see ways to meld the strengths of the genres into a whole that is, one hopes, more than the sum of its parts.

Finally, you have to live a life of broad interests. You can't acquire the breadth of experience that makes for good writing if you spend most of your weekends at writer-fan conventions. Get out, get around. See and do!

DEAN KOONTZ

Barry Malzberg said the reason he wrote science fiction was because he wanted to make sure he got into print. I think that once you get into a genre, you discover how rich it is, and how varied it is. And just how much you can do with it! And of course you gravitate toward that genre to which you feel close to anyhow, so it's not an act of "hackery."

It's an act of prudence.

PETER STRAUB

Try not to ape what other writers do.

You can model yourself on other writers, but don't ape what they do. For example, I loved Lovecraft's "At the Mountains of Madness." I loved the mythos. I loved the setting. I loved the story. I knew that I wanted to play with those elements someday. So when the time came for me to do my novel *Midsummer*, I did a story that starts off in Antarctica, moves to a small town in New York, has ties with these other-worldly creatures who have affected the characters there in Antarctica, and now, back here. But I don't think anyone who reads that book would flash on to the fact—outside of the Antarctica kick-off—that it owes a tremendous debt to Lovecraft. Because I filtered it through my *own* personal fear and concern center; the things I alone wanted to write about.

So if you do have models—if you have writers whose work you've enjoyed and have inspired you—make sure that your writing becomes *personalized*. That will have some truth to you in the sense that you write about what has scared *you*, and you'll base your writings on the experiences in life that *you've* had.

Or you've been scared for your children, and you're going to convey that feeling in this novel or story when you're writing about children.

Or it's you who've hiked into the deep woods and spent the night there being scared, and now you're going to take that feeling and use it if you're dealing with a character . . . who's loose in the woods and tracking you down.

MATTHEW J. COSTELLO

Anybody who tries to manipulate the market by saying, "I know what people want to read," and writes a novel on that preconception of mass appeal is probably going to fail. You shouldn't cynically write a novel about something that is of current interest. Because interests change rapidly, and by the time your book is written and published, public fascination with that subject could be so outmoded that nobody cares! More than that, I think readers smell a fake when they pick up a book. They can tell that a writer didn't really believe in the book, that the writer was just trying to cash in on a trend. You really have to follow your own voice. You have to be yourself when you write. In effect, you have to announce, "This is me, this is what I stand for, this is what you get when you read me. I'm doing the best I can—buy me or not—but this is who I am as a writer."

DAVID MORRELL

I try not to write about subjects I don't have first-hand knowledge of. For example, about ten years ago I had a great idea for a novel set in Viet Nam. But I missed that war. I figured no amount of research was going to give that story the ring of truth, so I didn't do it. I think it's okay to just write about the areas in which you've lived, and the type of people you've been surrounded with in those areas. You get closer to describing things the way they really are, rather than hoping for the best by doing a lot of research where you don't have any personal experiences.

RICHARD LAYMON

Each one gets harder! You always want to do a little better than last time, and . . . it just gets a little more difficult to do something new, something different. You don't want to start repeating yourself. I always thought that once I got past the first couple of books it would get easier, and I keep waiting for it to happen. But it never does.

WHITLEY STRIEBER

I know too many people who make the corrections on the screen without printing out that draft. They'll lock in those corrections, print it out, and then later say, "Now wasn't there a wonderful paragraph here before?" So I always print out my "junk" manuscripts. I may have 2,000 pages of junk manuscript piled beside my desk, but when I get into revisions, I can say, "Hey, there *was* a great paragraph there before." I'll get down on my hands and knees and go through pages and pages until I often find something I should not have cut.

And I'll put it back in.

DAVID MORRELL

I never separate one form of art from another; I've never seen it that way. I approach writing a short story in much the same way as all these other things that I do, by first scheduling it in to my work schedule. I feel better—or less at risk—when I've got a structure ready and some sort of finish; but I don't restrict myself to that outline. If a better finish presents itself, which it sometimes certainly does, then I'll abandon the original one.

GAHAN WILSON

Sometimes there are legitimate reasons for using them. If your publisher wants you to have only one book a year under your name, yet you have the ability to write two, you might need a pen-name. But I also used them for the wrong reason, because of bad advice. I wrote in a wide range of styles, and I experimented with style, so I was told that every time I did something different from what I'd done before, I had to use to a different name in order not to alienate or confuse the reader. After a while I figured out this wasn't true; readers will stay with an author, no matter what the variations in style and genre, as long as they get that sense of story, of character, of empathetic involvement that the work provides when it's functioning at its highest level.

In fact I've learned that readers appreciate a writer who will risk fresh approaches, book after book—as long as the stretch the writer is making actually works. I began to realize that all these books, which were being well reviewed under pen names, were doing absolutely nothing to build *my* name. Nobody knew those writers were me! If all the books had been published under one byline, and those good reviews had reflected upon me—not upon a motley group of pseud-onyms—the reading public would have been aware of me far sooner. So I dropped all of them.

DEAN KOONTZ

For those who at this point have to depend on some other means of making a living, I would say to them that they should try to find enough time to write a page or even half a page a day. Because if you did just a page a day, at the end of the year you'd have 365 pages. And if you managed to do five pages a day, think of the amount of pages you'd have at the end of the year! Now forget for the moment that you have to revise those pages at some point, or that research may have to be done on a project. What's important to remember is that you're not writing a long book—you're just writing a certain number of pages each day . . . A novel gets done by persistence, by emphasizing a short-term daily goal that makes a long-term goal seem less daunting.

DAVID MORRELL

If you're talking about advice to young writers, it's simply to write. Write all the time. The more you write, the easier it becomes. It's still hard work. It'll always be hard work!

MICHAEL MCDOWELL

[My advice to anyone considering the writers life:] Learn to be a plumber. I'm serious. You need to learn something where you can make money, set your own hours, and then spend your spare time writing as you see fit. A plumber makes pretty good wages, doesn't have to work all the time, and doesn't have to take a specific job if he doesn't want to. I was a janitor, and found that was good for me. The rest of the advice is put your ass in a chair, put some paper in a typewriter, and write.

JOE R. LANSDALE

One practical way of making the leap from genre to mainstream, without sacrificing your principles is to think *bigger*. Dan Simmons's *Carrion Comfort* is a perfect example of what I'm taking about. After Stephen King's *'Salem's Lot*, one would have thought that the vampire story had more or less been exhausted. *Carrion Comfort* was first published as a thirty page short story. Then Simmons developed it into a novel that's big enough to give you a hernia! But the novel isn't just big—it's fresh, it's ambitious, it's inventive. So I would tell any genre novelist that if your manuscript is less than 300 pages, it's too short. I don't know any major publisher who will give a genre book a push—will treat it as important—unless the manuscript runs about 600 pages. But that many pages doesn't mean simply more words. There has to be more incident and, above all, a vision as big as the book.

DAVID MORRELL

You always risk the danger of your pen-name becoming more famous than your own. Two of my first three, million-seller paperbacks were under other names. And look at Evan Hunter. He's a wonderful novelist, but more people know "Ed McBain" than know Evan Hunter now. The first book I had on any best-seller list was *The Key to Midnight* by Leigh Nichols. And *that* was an unsettling event, because I couldn't go around in bookstores grabbing people and saying "Hey, this Nichols is really me!" I'd look deranged! The second was *Whispers*, which was under my own name, but then the third was *The Funhouse* under the "Owen West" identity. I now recommend that writers avoid pen names. If you have to pay the bills, and you write something you're not proud of, use a pen-name for that. But if you're proud of your books—as I was of those under many of my pseudonyms—put them out under your name and to hell with what the wisdom of the business is!

Because if the books are written with care and passion, publishing them under other identities softens your impact. And if you want

to publish two books a year under your own name and your publisher doesn't, maybe you need a new publisher.
DEAN KOONTZ

You do the best job you can on whatever the hell it is you're doing, but you should *always* let it rest, and then go back and do it better than before. "Let's improve the damn thing one more time before we throw it out there!" And sometimes you improve it quite dramatically.
GAHAN WILSON

Because of certain things that happened to me when I was very young, I grew up a loner and an outsider and I found myself tapping into those feelings more and more as my writing career went along. I had to learn how to be truthful with myself as a writer. Hemingway told Fitzgerald not to drink his pain but to use it as writing, and while that sounds like one of those calculatedly macho things Ernie was given to saying, I think there's truth in it: a lot of us have to learn how to quit bullshitting ourselves at the word processor. Otherwise, you spend your years turning out very sleek but empty pieces of work.
ED GORMAN

I know that as much as I don't like to sit down some mornings and look at that word processor, still the pages will happen. (I'm all for word processors; writing is a damn chore no matter what, and anything you can find to make it easier, latch on to it. Can you imagine how it was when they wrote with a quill pen?) You should have a routine and no expectations. Just see what happens.
JOHN FARRIS

I never send [the completed work] out unless I can give myself a chill. As my agent has told me, I write word by word. *Every* single word has to count—even in the novels. Every word in the book has to work toward *that last line*. Like on *The Pet*, I worked on the last scene for I don't know how long to get it just *right*. Only then was I ready to send in the manuscript. I still have to go . . . [breaks into maniacal laughter] . . . or I won't send it out.
CHARLES L. GRANT

Some of the rejections I received for *Interview with the Vampire* were ludicrous. Fortunately I was confident enough to know that they were ludicrous. Somebody else might have been hurt and quit. But I kept writing, and kept mailing out. My attitude was, "I'm going to become a writer." I *was* a writer.

So my advice is to remember that you're dealing with people who make decisions on the basis of a whim, and just *keep going*. Keep going until you connect with a person who cares enough about what you've done to publish it. And don't be discouraged if you hit twenty people who aren't that one.

ANNE RICE

Don't try and copy someone else's work but use it to inspire your own development as a writer. Keep the inspiration level high, and the actual mimicry level low.

MATTHEW J. COSTELLO

Oh, it has to be like a nine to five day! A free-lancer has *got* to be enormously disciplined. I work very hard. Oh God, I start sometimes at seven-thirty or eight in the morning, and almost always put in a full day, with a little dinky lunch break. But I always have the option—which is very nice!—of saying, "Screw it! Today I'm not going to work." Or I'll take an afternoon off.

But you've got to *do* it; you've got to be sure to accomplish what is owed, or it's just not going to work. And it gets complicated, because there's always other projects going on—movies, writing. It's a terrific balancing act because you have to make sure you don't shortchange any particular project. Because if you do, it shows.

GAHAN WILSON

Never, never try to scope the market. If you say, "They want science fiction, so I'll write science fiction," or "they want mysteries so I'll write mysteries," then you're *doomed*. You've got to write what you're passionate about. Otherwise you'll produce juiceless, flavorless fiction. I sold my first story when I was a senior in college, and to some extent I regret that I started selling so young. Because "young" and "naive" are two words which go together, as are "young" and "stupid"—at least in my case.

A lot of that early work is so poorly formed because I was inexperienced and floundering, but I *was* passionate, all right. Because I began that early, I was writing what I'd read as a kid, which

was science fiction. It was my favorite form of fiction then, so I wrote it out of sheer love. But I eventually burnt out on it.
DEAN KOONTZ

There has to be a basic *simpatico*, and an intellectual joining, for you to [collaborate] in the first place. The easy stage, the fun stage, is putting the story together, when you're just throwing story ideas back and forth and constructing a story. It's when you get to the actual writing that there's liable to be some difference in your approaches, because nobody writes the same way. Nobody hears things the same way in their minds.
RICHARD MATHESON

I'll tell you, on the face of it, collaborating is *the* most complicated process in the world. Having worked with Mick Garris, my Dad, and some other people, either you can collaborate—or you can't. It's almost like a really good conversation with somebody that you've just met. It either falls into place or it doesn't. You think back and say, "How on earth did that happen? We talked about all these personal, complicated subjects, and yet it felt natural and it felt perfect." Or you think about other conversations, and you say, "God, it was just painful to try and get through that." And that's the way it is with collaboration. It is not a perfect process, but either you see things alike, or you do not.
RICHARD CHRISTIAN MATHESON

You spend a *lot* of time thinking about where the next book is going to come from. All told, I've got about 30 books out. And each time you do one, you use up—not just your main idea—but all kinds of ideas and concepts and memories. I might hit the bottom of the barrel at some point. But I think it's your attitude—as long you don't think there'll ever be a bottom of the barrel, there won't be! And there's always new ways of looking at subjects, no matter how many times they've been done.
RICHARD LAYMON

Ultimately, if you're going to make a living as a writer, you're going to have to make that jump where you say: "Okay, I know my interests, I have my craft. And I know one other thing: I know the history of my genre." Too many writers don't know the traditions of their specialty. In my own case, new thrillers. I read what amounts to the first few pages to determine whether or not I want to take this one home, because I'm *still* keeping up with the field. And it amazes me how many of the books sound as if they were written by the same author. They frequently have the same kind of deadness of tone. The authors have no sense of storytelling, no sense of announcing, "Hey, I've got something special to tell you!" Whenever a novice writer discovers that—whatever that missing magic is which makes a novel special—then that writer's innocence disappears, and he or she is ready to become a professional. Each writer has to discover a unique approach to technique and subject that is his or hers alone.

DAVID MORRELL

It's very important to have an agent, but I think it's easier to get an editor the first time out. Because agents have to make a living, and editors really don't. In other words, they get paid whether they publish you or somebody else. So with that first novel—especially if it's a passionate, literary novel—it may be easier to get an editor at a good literary house than it is to get an agent. Because most agents just have to be more commercial to survive. I say, if you can get an agent, fine, but don't wait for one. I'd go after both at the same time. If it's plainly a more commercial book, agents may look kindly on it right away. But the main thing to remember is that you can't take seriously anything these people say because they're *not* writers.

The point to remember is that many of them, no matter how hard working they may be, are not very nice people. You can't be hurt by them. Just because somebody has a sign that says "Editor," and has paid vacation and medical insurance and works for a publishing company, doesn't necessarily mean that that person knows very much or is very smart or is worth listening to. So don't take it seriously if they brush off your manuscript with a couple of lines.

ANNE RICE

Avoid the obvious. Go for the personal.

Make it something that disturbs YOU. If it is something that disturbs and unnerves you, it is far more likely to affect the reader. It is in the practicing of your craft that you learn to take things that are very personal to you and then express them, with enough clarity and power, so that your audience not just sees, not just reads whatever it is you just wrote down, but *experiences* it on some level.

STEPHEN R. BISSETTE

Be original as you can—but be true to yourself. Your story may not be the most original story in the world. But if it has that truth where it is directly connected to you, and you relate to what you're writing about, and you tap into your own fears, then that story—even if it's covering some familiar ground—will have power and resonance. But it must be filtered through your own personality.
MATTHEW J. COSTELLO

Besides all the good advice he's given me over the years, Dean Koontz's also been a role model in terms of a what a writer can do, the limits he can push beyond. He'll make up his mind he's going to do something, and then he'll just go ahead and do it. He's also been rewriting a lot of his old books, and making a lot more money from republishing them now than when they were first published. And that is something every writer should keep in mind: *your old stuff can still be very valuable.* As soon as you have something published, if you can get the rights back, get the rights back! Because, later on, that material might be worth considerably more than it was when it was first published.
RICHARD LAYMON

Basically, persist. And if anybody asked me, I would do my best to discourage them, because if I *could* discourage them, then they've got no business doing it because they're going against incredible odds. And they have to be half mad to think they can succeed. I was. I am! Anybody in the arts is. It's impossible to succeed. It's like winning the lottery. Forget it—out of the question. And it's a heart-breaker. Artists always make a big deal out of that—but so is life!
GAHAN WILSON

You have to think—to trick yourself into believing—"I'm the best writer I know." You *have* to think that way. If you think you're lousy, you'll never improve, never get anywhere. In other words, you have to *believe in yourself.*
CHARLES L. GRANT

This is something I've learned, but I have to keep reminding myself that I know it. And that is, in many ways, the publishing industry is really impersonal. That acceptances and rejections by agents and editors really, in many cases, have very little to do with the individual writer or the quality of his or her writing. A lot of it just has to do with compatibility—what the agents and editors are looking for at that time. So as discouraging as it may be to have your book turned down a number of times, it *doesn't* mean that it's a bad book. It just might be that hundreds of thousands of people would enjoy it, if they just had the chance to read it. But [your book] never had its chance from the start simply because it didn't reach an enthusiastic person in the industry. So it's often a compatibility issue, not a quality issue.

JOSEPH A. CITRO

It's always a tempting technique when you're starting out to be a writer. You start with the ending of the story. "Wouldn't it be cool if. . . ?" and work back from there. Or you think of a real gross thing that could happen, and then try to build a story towards that. And basically the entire story hangs on getting to that twist ending. Sometimes it works. Look at Robert Bloch—he did so many of them! But it's not the ending that really counts. Because the ending doesn't work unless you've done all the work beforehand to make it count. So just having a great [shock] ending isn't enough. You have to build up to it; you have to make the ending integral to the story and the characters. And you can't tip your hand—with a lot of these kind of stories you can see the ending coming a mile away.

F. PAUL WILSON

When I'm editing anthologies, the biggest mistake [new contributors] make is that they think they have to "trick" the reader. You know? When you get to the last page of the story . . . oh, no! . . . "it was a vampire!" Or . . . "it wasn't dead!" Or . . . "he was a she!" But when it's a really well crafted story, you don't have to be "tricked." You know you're being manipulated from the first paragraph—*but you don't care!* Because it feels right. Because it works. Because the writer makes you immediately believe in the whole scenario.

But when you get to the end of a story like that, and if you haven't already guessed the "surprise" ending—which you usually have!—you feel . . . cheated. In order to be surprised by a trick ending you can't have been given all the necessary information. Only a real master of the form can do that—where he lays it all in and you just don't see it because it's in the trees instead of the forest!

But most writers who are just getting started are cheating the

reader, and cheating themselves, because they're not yet following the rules of good storytelling.
THOMAS F. MONTELEONE

My theory is that if you're easily discouraged, you'd better not try to be a writer! You just keep on going, no matter how bad everyone says your work is, and no matter how many people say, "You really have to face up to reality: You just can't do this."
JOHN SAUL

It's hard work. The more you do, the more you push yourself. A couple of years ago I came to the realization that I am never going to be content in life. Because I am always going to be trying to do something a little better than I did before. This is not the kind of thing where you can build your career by going up through sales and marketing, and then you're vice president, and if you're a good boy and the company doesn't fold you can retire with a great pension.

In this line of work, you're only as good as your last book.

And your next book.
CHET WILLIAMSON

Not being one to give advice, I'll only say always write the best that you can. Whether it's a short story or a novel or whatever, just do the best you possibly can. Because it's through your words that people are going to know you, and like ghosts, your words can come back to haunt you.
JOSEPH A. CITRO

I've always been suspicious of the rule, "Write what you know about." I've always felt one should "write about what you'd *like* to know about." That's why I've always preferred stories that are un-usual, and that are out of the mainstream. I'm writing novels I can't find to read elsewhere. And when they are really working well, they surprise *me* while I'm writing them.

Usually I have to have the ending in mind, and the beginning, and then I work out how I'm going to get from point A to point Z. I remember when I started *Deathtrap*, I had no idea of what was going to happen in the second act. I knew how I wanted to end up—with the two main characters destroying each other— but I had no idea how or why to get there. And then there was this moment when I was writing halfway through act one when I realized that Clifford in act two would be writing a tell-all play called "Deathtrap." I remember just jumping out of my chair with delight. It was such a total surprise to me, as it was when Sidney, the playwright in the play, discovered this horrible turn of events.

Those are the best moments—when I'm surprised in the same way I hope the reader will be.

IRA LEVIN

When I was starting as a writer, people were always saying, "Well, how long are you going to give it?" And, "When are you going to get a job?" I would just stare at them blankly. It's ones who send me letters asking "Tell me how to get started." *They're* the ones who are in trouble! I never asked anybody how to get started! I corresponded in the early days with Ray Bradbury, but only to tell him how much I liked his work, and he wrote me back telling me how much he enjoyed my early short stories. But I wasn't asking for advice on how to become a writer.

There is no big secret. Just keep writing. And keep writing about the things you feel strongly about. You should not write anything that doesn't absolutely turn you on; that you *love*. I *love* writing. It's a hard field. It's very often unrewarding financially—and certainly cre-atively—for the majority. But if you *do* love it, great. Stay with it! You should love any field you go into. I love it, and I will stay in it until the day I die.

RICHARD MATHESON

CHAPTER TEN

The Function and Importance
of Unpleasant Truths

It's just that people have to have this stuff. You need it—like a little salt in your diet.

Stephen King

Although I don't personally believe this, I like the idea that the mind is strong enough to create something nasty and external. But it all comes from the mind. And we live in pretty damn horrible times. I mean, some nasty things are happening out there. Horror, just like every other popular art, is a reflection of the times. We don't create these monsters; society creates them, and we just reflect them in our work.

You've got to go through the darkness before you can come out into the light. I would use the term "shadows to illuminate." There are exceptions, but most of what I've written—in the books anyway—end on a note of triumph or hope. At least hope.

If there's not hope ... if a novel is absolutely full of despair and nothing else, I really wouldn't want to read it. *"We go through hell to get to heaven."* But there is the question: what if some readers can't see *that*. "I read it for the *good* parts." But you can't let that stop you from doing what you want to do.

Chet Williamson

One always has to look at art as having function. Art is not *ever* to be dismissed as "escapism." I'm hugely preoccupied with the idea of claiming *fantastique* back from the critics and academics who would dismiss it as being escapist and useless. It's very important to reiterate how significant and rich that tradition is, because those of us who are "in the genre," the *fantastique* genre—and by that I mean horror fiction, and speculative fiction, high fantasy—that whole area of imaginative fiction, we are vulnerable to critical attitudes that will dismiss anything which is not "naturalistic" or "realistic."

If we were writing in translation, if we were South American "magic realists" of course this wouldn't be a problem, because they have such intellectual respect there. But that attitude doesn't take into account the rich and diverse work which is being done at the moment—and which has *always* been done—in this area.

CLIVE BARKER

I think [horror is] a perfectly acceptable art form. One of the most accepted literary forms is the Elizabethan drama, and God knows that's just *full* of gore! In Marlowe, and Shakespeare, and so forth, you've got people squeezing other people's eyeballs out, and inflicting ghastly tortures on one another—just total *Grand Guignol*. And Grand Guignol has always been an accepted art form. And visually, in the history of art, the church adored paintings of the saints being hideously mutilated. Paintings done by absolutely marvelous painters—practically every classical painter has done the crucifixion of Christ, which is one of the most ghastly torture scenes there is.

Horror movies have never been the Main Tent—they've always been the sideshow. And serious critical attention has come to very few of them. Usually when they're long gone, and they've become relics, and their historical importance has become obvious. It's the same as in literature: H.G. Wells is still read. He's there; he's a fixture. And Edgar Allan Poe . . . and Nathaniel Hawthorne. No matter how many times somebody might try to second-rate them, they're now accepted. But with very rare exceptions, horror movies and spooky stuff in the theatre have never been accepted as respectable. But that's very much part of their appeal.

GAHAN WILSON

A story like "Hansel and Gretel" is as direct and as powerful a tool as saying to your child repeatedly, "Don't put your hand on that burner. It will hurt you." Our kids *are* going to put their hands on that burner if we insist in telling them that in "Hansel and Gretel" the witch is not really bad, she does not eat children, and that Hansel and Gretel do not have to kill the witch to escape. There are certain hard facts of life which are coded into those fairy tales that we grew up with.

When we were kids they were not treated as horror tales, at all, but "Hansel and Gretel" is a horror story! "Pinocchio" is a horror story! "The Wizard of Oz" is a terrifying horror story! And the reason these "fairy tales" have lasted so long is because there are real truths in there. And those truths are just as relevant today, if not more so, as they were when the Brothers Grimm put pen to paper and wrote down the folk tales they had grown up with. Call them what you will, these are important tools which should be used by every successive generation of parents.

STEPHEN R. BISSETTE

Warday takes the movement the farthest it's ever gone—I don't think there's ever been a horror novel as vitally connected to the issues and the reality of terror in our time. Horror fiction is uniquely capable of dealing with the *real* nightmares of this period; there isn't another form of literature that is capable of doing it. If we're going to learn to be able to grapple consciously with these terrors, it's going to be through the medium of horror fiction.

WHITLEY STRIEBER

I've always thought that the real advantage to the kind of books we write—over other genres—is that they have a deep vein of surrealism in them. It's that aspect of the field that I really find most valuable. I don't mean that in any pretentious way, but I mean that in the heart of very good books in the "Gothic" manner, there is this basic question about the nature of reality. Like the juxtaposition in Magritte of two ordinary things that creates some kind of spark of disquiet and unease. There is a shaking up of the material world that supernatural fiction *has* to do—it has to jolt reality, and slice into it.

Insanity *is* real, actual horror. And of course a depiction of it only works if it's coming as much from inside the characters as from outside. It really must do that, or it's childish. There has to be some kind of "echo" in the characters of the basic situation, and there has to be some kind of "rhyme" between the situation and the characters. I think you really should have characters for whom you feel deeply, since you want to have characters who have "worlds" inside them, because everybody you know has a world inside them. And you want these people to be as complete as possible—and *then* subject them to whatever godawful thing you subject them to!

PETER STRAUB

It's the greatest creative profession. Anyone can do it any time. Unlike moviemaking, dancing, and classical music, painting—anything at all—writing requires a minimum of equipment, yet allows for a maximum expression of passion and creativity.

You can do it at the kitchen table on paper you stole from the office with an old typewriter you got at a junkstore. And you can make it from there to the bestseller lists. Somebody does that just about every year. Like Judith Guest, the housewife from Ohio who wrote *Ordinary People* and sent it in over the transom.

The important thing to remember is that it is an artistic realm—even if you're writing the most commercial fiction or non-fiction. That means there's no justice. It doesn't matter how hard you work, it doesn't matter who you know. What ultimately matters is what you put on that page—and whether somebody wants it at the moment. That's when anyone who wants to go into this profession has to a) believe in themselves totally, b) work like a demon, and c) ignore the rejections.

ANNE RICE

Horror fiction has as its basis the human condition, and it can talk about that condition in a way that other types of fiction cannot. It's the idea that this literature that we do has worth—it's also fun, it's a hell of a lot of fun!—but it has *worth*. And I think it has enduring worth. People are beginning to realize that as well, and they're reading horror now as serious literature. . . . The longest running tradition in literature is the horror tale, and it goes back to *Beowolf*, and I'm sure it goes back to the oral tales of "You better not go by the swamp, because there's something in there." These tales of warning, of danger—either in a physical or a mental way—which show the ways others have dealt with it, have been around a long, long, time. And will be around until the end of time.

ROBERT R. McCAMMON

I don't think there's a simple answer. We know there's been an enthusiasm for this kind of material since a group of higher primates sat around a fire together, and told each other ghost stories. I can imagine that the first conversation was something like, "Gee, I'm glad we've got fire. But doesn't it make the darkness even . . . darker?"

I think we've answered the question right there.

CLIVE BARKER

Maybe that's the next step for me, to *really* get as far as I can in presenting Evil as it really is. Evil is such a tenuous thing; in some sense it's very, very subtle, and in other ways it's very obvious and very overt. It's a wonderful, mysterious, mystical area. And that's why we do it. That's why we keep striving to reach for that understanding.

JAMES HERBERT

People who criticize horror films are not acknowledging that part of life, or that part of themselves. I firmly believe that every human being has the capacity for madness and wildness in them, and horror films express this—I think—in usually a very harmless way.

I don't think of horror films as instigation [of violence in our society]; I think of them as reflections. In general art is like that. It's funny, because art is always the first thing that is attacked. I think this is because the arts reflect events so truly, it's frightening. Horror films often reflect a truth that is too unpalatable for the society at large, especially for the political leaders, to be really comfortable with. Like it or not, we live in a lethal world. From what I can see of our culture and civilization, it is shot through with wars, and murders, and tortures—a truly great amount of terrifying horror. The threat of atomic warfare has been with us all our lives, to say nothing of germ warfare or biological warfare. People don't want to talk about this, but it's always there.

This is the amazing thing of denial that I'm continually struck by: that people never mention the actual, real horrors in our world when they criticize horror films. They'd rather blame the horror film for influencing or "damaging" their children. But these are kids who are growing up with junkies in the forth grade, you know? People are coming into their schools carrying AK-47 assault rifles, or sniping at them from rooftops. It's on the news nightly for these kids to see. It's not like the horror film is introducing them to something that's never occurred to them!

The reason some of these kids walk around with Freddy Krueger dolls is the same reason that horror filmmakers are a little bit more relaxed about the terrors around us, because they are able to handle it, manipulate it, and call it their own for the moment. That's what a child does with a Freddy Krueger doll. That's what a teenager does with a horror film: they're somehow able to identify with it, and say "This I can handle. The person who I identify most with in this film probably will survive." Most horror films, no matter how devastating the action may become, are usually hopeful in the end, with the person you identify with most *surviving*.

WES CRAVEN

In a larger sense, we may all be spending our entire lives writing only one story, the finest story we know: one with ourselves as hero rather than victim or arch-enemy. As D.W. Griffith said, "What you get is a living, what you give is a life." It's up to each of us to try and make it worth reading— or living.

DENNIS ETCHISON

First of all, scaring people *is* entertaining them. Fear is a powerful, visceral, and perversely *fun* kind of emotion. Especially if you know you can get out of the frightening situation just by closing the book or walking out of the theater.

GARY BRANDNER

I remember being on a panel back at the very first World Fantasy Convention. And among the very illustrious people on the panel was dear old Manly Wade Wellman. And somebody asked all of us "Why do you like to do these things that frighten people?" So we all sort of stalled around one way or another, and some tried to answer profoundly, but Manly had the best answer. He said when he was a kid, he remembered they'd be out there in the woods, and sitting around a fire. And he'd start to tell a story, and he'd make it scarier, and scarier, and scarier. And he said, "Their eyes would pop. I loved to make their eyes . . . pop!" Then he paused and said, "I still do—I love to make their eyes . . . pop!"

And that's true for me.

GAHAN WILSON

The theory in the past, when these stories were popular in the Victorian era and afterwards, was that there were a lot of sexual symbolism, and sexual metaphors of people creeping into each other's rooms and doing these things to one another. Although there's still some of that, vampires now relate more directly to the immortality concept. The idea that people have of maintaining their bodies forever, which is now part of our public consciousness in weird, desperate ways such as diets and exercise. People assume if they do these things, they will somehow cheat death. I think the appeal of vampires today has something to do with that idea. My vampire characters do pay a price to be vampires. And part of that price is that they are predators. I suppose that's a more traditional approach. I'm ambivalent as to whether they're "admirable" or not—they always have a cruel and inhuman streak in addition to the advantages they obviously possess. The one advantage that interests me the most is not just extending their current life, but the idea that, by being a vampire, they have acquired mystical knowledge about the meaning of life and death, and the beyond, and the secrets of the universe. That's very attractive to me, though it's still sort of a Faustian theme the way my vampires are paying for this. They are suffering, and they are causing suffering, in order to maintain their existence.

LES DANIELS

Books—the word on the printed page—carry an *immense* power to influence and will, in turn, generate other media events. Edgar Allan Poe, although he wrote a relatively small amount of material, has been transferred into movies, comic books, cartoons, and musicals, plays, television, and so on. You've got to look at that collective influence, and that is *enormous*.

CLIVE BARKER

I am someone who is constantly drawn to horror as a way of dancing on the edge of a cliff. It is an edge where none of us wants to go to in our real life; but in our imaginative lives, if we're drawn to horror as a genre, then we look to get as close to that abyss as we can. Some of the most powerful glimpses into that abyss are often buried in the midst of what most people would consider absolute trash.

STEPHEN R. BISSETTE

I find one of the dangers nowadays is that we can get very pompous about what we do. It's almost a defense mechanism. When people want to put down horror, we tend to try and explain it too much, and give too much motivation for what we're doing. I think we do it by instinct alone.

It's something that's within us. . . . I have great difficulty explaining what I do. I work by instinct. Others are very articulate about this, but I try not to be. I really try not to be. Because I don't want to open that box. I don't want to see the mechanics of it.

I don't know how the tricks work! And I'm determined to keep it that way. I'm a magician by instinct. To me, it is magical. In the true sense. Writing is not a mechanical thing; it's not trickery. And as soon as you analyze, and as soon as you give reasons, and as soon as you get pretentious about it, or try to explain it, I think it evaporates. It disappears.

JAMES HERBERT

Most of great literature uses the resources of horror, uses the basic elements of horror, to bring home its point. Tapping into that primal notion of fear is something all great writers have done. It would be redundant to say that Shakespeare's done it; any great work of fiction is probably going to have its moments where it is making use of that resource. What we as writers have done is kind of specialized in it, and that's okay, because we enjoy it and relish it so much, we want to play in that field all the time. But I think all great fiction has tapped into it to bring home the central conditions of fear and loss in the human condition.

MATTHEW J. COSTELLO

Writing about the unholy is one way to write about what's sacred.

CLIVE BARKER

I have the greatest affection for monsters. And I think it speaks to the idea that we are all "monstrous," that we aren't perfect, and that we have to accept that with grace and amusement. It's an absolutely *horrifying* world, and dreadful things are always happening. And you've got to be able to deal with it. And if you can deal with it with gentleness, with a lack of hatred, that's all to the good. *But you've got to learn how to handle it.* Monsters and horror are really a kind of primer on how to handle these things.

GAHAN WILSON

I don't think I or my colleagues could write horror if we didn't think it was a serious subject. I take it as a great insult when somebody says, "When are you going to write something serious?" But this *is* real—it's about life and death. You know, people who ask that question have never read horror—they don't know a damn thing about it! And they probably don't know much about... anything. Because horror writing has always seemed to me a very liberal, forward-thinking kind of literature that is not afraid to shake things up. It's not afraid to be nasty. It's not afraid. *It's just not afraid.*

And isn't that what art is all about? Horror fiction can be—is—art. Now "Art" may not necessarily be pleasant or nice to look at. And yet, to me, the beauty of horror is that there's so many ways to go, there's so many areas still left undiscovered and unexplored.

ROBERT R. MCCAMMON

I like black humor—I'm very attracted to it. And I think it's important in the kinds of books that we do to leaven them with some kind of humor, otherwise it just becomes *too* grim.

JACK KETCHUM

Maybe [creating fictional horror is] some sort of exorcism of the way you really feel about the horrors of life so that you can control it. Personally I've felt, quite often in my life, helpless in the face of the overwhelming weight of the world itself. I know that by making films like these, I at least have some sort of handle on it. Almost giving myself some sort of shield... so people will perceive me as being capable of frightening actions... and therefore they leave me alone.

WES CRAVEN

People turn to the arts and entertainment in general in search of a certain comfort, a certain predictability. But the point of horror is to go against the grain, to *not* make people comfortable. We want you to read something you've never read before! As writers, we want to stretch the boundaries of the genre. And if you're not willing to do that, you're doing the whole field a disservice, not just yourself. You're not trying to become a part of this great tradition, which is what makes horror so wonderful. Because it does disturb you. Because it does make you think differently. Because as a form of literature it *does its job!*

It's a lot easier to go for the quick shock, the cheap shot. I hope none of us ever do. The temptation is always there. But that's the greatest challenge in this field. Not to get comfortable and write the same serial killer or vampire story over and over again. My God, what are we here for as writers? We're here to shake the reader up. We're not here to make anyone comfortable.

THOMAS F. MONTELEONE

Although some publishers may treat it as a second-rate literature, it is a first-rate literature, as far as I'm concerned. I don't believe there's any other kind of literature that has as much to say, or is as strong. Or as important. I think many more people should be exposed to the genre. Because when you consider the term "horror fiction," the average person says, "Well, it must be . . . horrible." Or, "Why should I want to read something that gives me nightmares?" But good horror fiction can be a wonderful way of stirring things up—of making you appreciate life all the more because there *is* so much death and suffering in this world.

ROBERT R. McCAMMON

[The horror genre] is *endlessly* fascinating, it really is. But there's a lot of humor in my books as well. So both ends fascinate me: humor and horror. And they often walk hand in hand. To put it more basically, I just find that you can write about a very mundane situation, and you can get into that; but after a while, it can become tedious for a writer—and certainly for a reader. When you find that boredom is approaching, you can take that mental leap—and invite the reader to take it with you—and take that one bound into horror that transcends everything you've written before that. You know, it really stops you getting bored with what you're doing. You're only limited by your own imagination. You can dig into areas that nobody else wants to dig into. Or they didn't used to want to—now everybody wants to! It gives you a lift. It gives you a metaphorical erection, if you like. It just gets the blood flowing and the thoughts flowing. It's wonderful.

JAMES HERBERT

I consider that everything that I do, and all my stories, are "cautionary tales." I try to look for trends or conditions in our society that are frightening or potentially disruptive. Or conditions which are actually already disruptive, and to point a well-trained eye in that direction. Another favorite theme of mine is superstitions, and the perversion of religions, which I think are one of the major causes for many of the evils in our society. I try to warn people about the ways

their minds can be swayed if they don't remember to think for themselves.
JOHN RUSSO

What most people find disturbing when they meet someone who creates horror and/or fiction is that they're such an ... ordinary person. We make our living exorcising and exercising our fears, and as a result, we're perhaps more [mentally] balanced than people who don't do this for a living or stretch those imaginative "muscles."
STEPHEN R. BISSETTE

I did an introduction for a book called *Famous Monsters Chronicles* edited by Dennis Daniel. I wrote how every major society throughout history—save for our own—have as part of their folklore various rites of passages. To get across the truths and insights that the adults want to get across to the young people and the children. And always a very important part of these folklores has been to teach them about "scariness." To teach them about death and how to deal with the reality of their mortality: "Life is tough, kid. I want you to get ready for it." They would gently introduce the child to dealing with these fears by presenting them with the elders acting as bogeyman. The children need help with coping with these issues, and they are presented with these "bogeymen" that are relatively easy to handle at this stage. And then the fears they represent are eventually intensified. We don't have that in our society. But it's something that *absolutely* has to be done nevertheless.

So what we did in our society was to have these horror movies and series, and what Forry Ackerman did with his magazine, *Famous Monsters of Filmland*, he acted as a sort of shaman-priest to the young people. Because then they could look at these horrible things safely, over and over again, and Forry would have these awful puns beneath the pictures. Where the monsters would say something funny. But the kids could really *look* at these things. And you slowly realized that it wasn't really "Count Dracula." It's just a kindly, aging Romanian gentleman with cigar breath and a bad accent. Or Forry would publish a "behind-the-scenes" article on how a monster was created. And so on. It was a really sweet, gentle way of introducing many of us to confronting our fears dealing with the real world.

And it worked.

The attitude of most people in the horror business is that the method I've just discussed does work. It's the *perception* of reality that's the thing. The bogeyman stuff is a *vital* growing-up exercise. First you handle the artificial fear situations; like being frightened in a darkened movie theater. You then become perceptive—you understand that Count Dracula is just old Bela Lugosi with his cigar breath. And when you understand make-believe horror, then you can go on to understand *real* horror.

The problem with someone who is truly mentally ill, who is a serial killer, is that they can never figure that out. They don't "get it." There's no difference in reality there. If you don't go through this growth experience, you won't ever understand that a real dead body is a real dead body. And you have to—because you're a living but yet distinctly mortal creature.

GAHAN WILSON

Part of the thrill of fantasy is that it does push to unrealistic extremes. In writing and drawing fantasy, I find that it can be *more* than real. I think it was Alfred Hitchcock who once remarked that melodrama was life with all the boring parts taken out. I think it's a natural function: part of what gives fantasy the punch or thrill is that it will terrify you by going beyond things you ordinarily see.

FRANK MILLER

Horror writers are approaching "real" horror, but we're doing it in a way that is, hopefully, artistic and civilized. And in an educated and thoughtful way. We're not glorifying madness or murder or child abuse or any other of our twentieth century horrors. We're simply trying to make sense out of the chaos, and in the process, exploring ourselves as well. We have to go all the way in, to conduct exploratory surgery. And some surgery is done with a laser, and some with a saw. We may not like what we find, but we still have to know what's there. For me, that has always been one of the valid reasons to write horror fiction.

ROBERT R. McCAMMON

It's a field which has room for *everything*. No matter what the author's particular world-view or political message, the horror novel has room for that. I like to think of the genre as a huge bag in which you can put anything you want—including a lot of nasty stuff.

[But] it's a good idea to also put in other layers to the story in addition to the scares. Although it may appear to make the books less horrifying, you can still have the same degree of scares, sadism, or whatever, but just have it in a book that now contains a lot of character development and plot twists. A book which actually might *say* something about the human experience. You then can have all the politics and social commentary—whatever you might want—right along with whatever you're using to try and scare the reader with.

RICHARD LAYMON

With horror, you can tell parables, and that's a lot harder to do with a straight thriller. It's much harder to take a parable and squeeze it into a real-life story. Whereas with supernatural material you can make anything happen so as to fit in the notion that you want to fit between the lines. You can go back and forth between the text and subtext much more freely! It's a bonus in this genre, which I rather freely have done over the years.

GEORGE A. ROMERO

For me, it's really talking about morality. We're really talking about not being infinite. It's an existential truth, it's very raw and real. It's a very basic one, which is often lost sight of with all the layers of cultural persiflage and complexity. I think we are really just talking about the mind that doesn't see why it shouldn't be infinite and eternal, and a body that tells you right from the beginning that you are very definitely finite and time bound. I really think it is the tension between those two things that is the subject of horror.

So that's why you get that incredible variety in horror, because given that morality is the *real* subject of horror, there are an infinite number of approaches you can take to that subject.

DAVID CRONENBERG

What horror writing is about, in my opinion, is this journey through the netherworld. We all come from somewhere, and we're all going somewhere—and we don't know where. And we're all frightened. Every one of us, in nightmares, have lived through this fear. Now someone with a uniquely terrible series of experiences like I've had, maybe has a special relationship with fear. But most people walking the street have had the Ultimate Fear. I certainly don't know anyone who can't look back on a nightmare, and even if it didn't make much sense, it still drew them to a level of ultimate terror. So we all know what it's about, we all know what the terror *is*.

Horror novels are important because they help us deal with this. "Mainstream" novels are generally a type of moral fiction that is about the consciousness of everyday life. Horror novels are about the *inner* consciousness; about extending consciousness into the dark places of the soul. The novelist is a guide through the netherworld, and in a good horror novel, the *reader* is the hero of the journey. Not the main characters who are acted upon by the disasters. Stephen King, for example: his best characters are always his victims. When you read his books, you find yourself literally the hero of the story in the sense that he is guiding you from event to event, deeper and deeper into this netherworld.

And guiding you out again, too. There are some son of bitches who leave you dangling in the darkness; people who really don't know what they're doing or just out for a kick. The old "hack 'em up and scare 'em" deal. I'm not interested in that. I'm interested in horror as a serious fictional form.

WHITLEY STRIEBER

Like it or not, there are many aspects of horror fiction which offer clear and very penetrating insights into the human condition. Yet I can see some very prim and proper person saying that "Horror fiction is no good, and it should be banned." And that's been said to me before. After I gave a speech, I once had a person stand up who was very upset and asked me: "Why was I forcing people to read this stuff?" And I said I wasn't forcing anyone to read it. Because there is nothing wrong with reading horror fiction!

One of the reasons I like it is because there *is* an element of hope in most horror fiction; it doesn't all have to be dark. It can be a glorious human transformation as well as an unfortunate fall from grace. And a climb *to* grace. And that's what I believe the best in horror fiction entails. I think that's fantastic—I think that's fabulous! Of course, nothing I could say would probably keep anybody from censoring horror. But it'll never be censored in this house.

ROBERT R. MCCAMMON

But it's the same business; I realized that Frankenstein's monster was small pickin's next to the atom bomb. You know, there's an endless range of quite horrible things going on. And I drafted them into the cartoons because they were so horrific. One of the aspects of this business is that humor allows you to examine topics that ordinarily you just blink and don't look at—*can't* look at. But humor kind of holds you steady and says, "There, there, you can look at it." So you *do* look at it. And in that way, it's helpful. So I was saying, "Look at it. *Look at it.*" And I still am, in various ways.

GAHAN WILSON

Horror is not a genre of time and place, such as the Western. Or the private eye novel, which is a restriction of character and situation; there's a mystery, and you have to solve it. Horror is more a genre of emotion, and the emotion of fear or terror can be expressed in an infinite number of ways, with an infinite number of characters, times, places, situations, and plots. So you're very free with what you want to do with it because you're dealing with an emotion—or set of emotions—and not just a situation or a character.

CHET WILLIAMSON

The great thing about horror is that most of it will never become respectable.

ROBERT R. McCAMMON

I've never tried to arrive at a definition of Horror. You know, in science fiction there's that famous quote from Damon Knight, who, as a critic, says "Science Fiction is where I happen to be pointing at the moment." But, unfortunately, I think through the years that if I had to point my finger at where horror is at the moment, I would point at the audience.

ROBERT BLOCH

By using the vocabulary of the genre, we can give shape to our own unspoken fears, our hidden desires; all things we're afraid to consider not only because they don't scare us, but also they make us feel very *small* as human beings. The power of horror and all its iconography is that it allows us to give shape to those feelings and fears. If you use horror as confessional fiction or as an excuse to wallow in "Oh, what a horrible life I've had!", what's the point? If the genre exists to give shape and form to horrors taken out of one's life, then I think it serves a very important function.

Monsters have always fascinated me because they embody and

personify issues we don't talk about. That's their fascination. That's why we love them. That's why we're afraid of them. That's why we can't shake them.

I have found horror to be a very powerful tool.

I've seen it in my children as they grow up. They have gone through periods where—through their drawings and the themes they write about—they're doing the same thing. Horror allows them to get through to another stage of development. I know that's how it functions for me in my life. It's absolutely crucial to me as a valid art form.

STEPHEN R. BISSETTE

In some sense, we *are* born "strange." I don't know why some kids grow up with a love for the weird and the macabre, while other kids have absolutely no interest in it. When we would go camping out in the woods as kids, I was always the one who would sit up and tell ghost stories before the fire.

It was like, that was our place; *that's* what we're here for.

THOMAS F. MONTELEONE

I've always thought that horror can address the question of evil in the world better than any other branch of fiction. Because we can personalize evil, we can make it incarnate, we can look at it from every angle. We can look at evil from the inside. And certainly the question of evil in the world is one of the most important questions that faces a human being. And I think we are the ones who have the ability to address this issue. *The Exorcist* was a novel that really wanted to examine the nature of evil and the possibility of transcendence. Those are heavy issues, and think it did it admirably. Even Dan Simmon's first novel, *Song of Kali*, took a moral stance and was very stylishly written.

Horror fiction puts human beings in a crucible and turns up the heat as no other fiction can do. In the sense that you can melt away all the little layers with which we coat ourselves, and get down to what's really underneath a character. What they're really made of. I can't think of any other genre where you can get the kind of "heat" that you can apply with horror fiction.

F. PAUL WILSON

Usually when I talk about fellow horror writers, I find that others ask me, "Aren't those people all *weird*???" It's amazing that most of the people in this field are so nice. And I think it's because we're able to get all this acid out on paper. To get these bad feelings and impulses out on paper, which so-called "normal" people can't do. Everybody has violent impulses sometimes, where they'd just like to rip somebody to pieces; where they're inflicted by some kind of momentary madness. But we can get it all out on paper. We're probably a lot more healthy, mentally, then a lot of these folks running around.

ROBERT R. McCAMMON

To my way of thinking, the most important aspect of a writer's work is to make the reader feel that they are "lost" in another world or reality, a sense of being taken away from their present circumstances—whatever they are—and *blasting* them somewhere else. That can—and does—happen in other genres.

What makes horror magical by comparison is that, if you read mysteries or suspense, you're reading the *story*. You're reading the *plot*. You're reading *character*. And the book will hold your interest based on how well all those elements are constructed.

But when you're reading horror—if the writer is doing his job—the reader bypasses that intellectual understanding and goes into something that is very, very primitive. Like when we huddled in caves around a fire and hoped that we could keep whatever was outside— outside. We go there again when we read horror. We're still huddling in caves: whether it's a gated community in La Jolla, California, or in a doorman-watched building on Park Avenue, or in a supposedly safe suburb in Westchester. We're still huddling, trying to keep the Bad Things out.

What horror does is bring it—the fears—back in, and by doing so really connects us with something that is very primitive and very primal about being a human being. About who we are—and where we came from.

Now, is that something that's "valuable" or "positive?" I think that anything that connects with something which is basic to the human condition, that makes us understand ourselves better, and empathizes with all of us, has its value.

That's the special voice that horror sings with.

MATTHEW J. COSTELLO

CHAPTER ELEVEN

"Where *DO* You Get Your Ideas?"

I agree with Ray Bradbury who says "idea is damn near everything."
Unfortunately, I found that a lot of my students believed that too
literally! The idea grabs them, and they simply dash through it, and I had
to kind of yell at them and say, "Back up, let's have some characters with
flesh on their bones—and remember to put a comma in occasionally."

Nonetheless, I think you have to gear yourself to making internal
connections, no matter where it is that you are. In the sense that a
doctor is always a doctor, no matter where he goes; a lawyer is always
a lawyer. I think a writer should always consider him or herself a
writer. Beyond the great importance of original idea, and the concept
of always thinking like a writer and living and working like a writer,
is the fact that writers *read*. People who say they want to write, I
believe, don't really read enough. And don't always read enough in
categories beyond which they want to write. You can't go on writing
forever about, say, vampires. Be aware of what's going on in the world;
be more aware of *many* topics to bring authenticity and verisimilitude
to your work. And if you don't have that, you may have to depend
solely on your idea—and that may not be enough.

The other thing is of course to write, write, write—then write
some more. Whether you send it out or not. You should also try to be
more self-critical. And if you're more self-critical of yourself now than
I was when I started my full-time career, you won't be submitting
material which is consistently, indubitably, unpublishable. Some of it
will finally be good, then.

J. N. WILLIAMSON

I know *exactly* where I got the idea [for my novel *Creature*]. I was watching the evening news about a year and a half ago, and there was a report on human growth hormones. The report got to talking in the future about "designer bodies." That there will come a time when you can pick your body style and there will be a combination of hormones that will allow you to have that body style. And I thought, "*That's* kind of creepy!" Two minutes later, I thought, "There's the idea for the next book. How is this all going to work?"

Immediately I saw one of those small towns where the major focus of everything is the high school football team, and *what if* one of these little towns figured out a way to make their team absolutely unbeatable?

Bingo!

JOHN SAUL

You read or see something, and suddenly you realize what you want to do. So I decided to break off from working on my witchcraft novel, now that I saw the whole philosophical sweep and philosophical conclusion of *Queen of the Damned*. A lot of this came into my head before I even wrote one word. Finally the time came when I couldn't afford to put it off any longer, and I sat down and wrote one word.

ANNE RICE

[I wrote *They Thirst* because] I always wanted to do a vampire novel. So I thought, where would be a good place to set a vampire novel? First it was going to be set in Chicago, and be about teen-age gangs who were vampires. I did two hundred pages of that book... and you get to a certain point where it either takes off or it doesn't take off. Well, that was one that *didn't* take off! I wanted an epic novel that I could take in a lot of different directions, so the first thing I did was have a detective who was originally from Hungary, who had a lot of prior experiences with these vampire forces. So, where? Los Angeles—a lot of different kinds of people out there, different nationalities. I mean, who says a vampire can't be Jewish, or whatever? So I went from there, and this time it worked out.

ROBERT R. McCAMMON

I have an idea for a new horror novel practically every day. I thought of one this morning, actually. A guy buys this old Zenith radio, and hears on it these old radio programs. He also hears the most grisly things going on, like he's witnessing these ritual murders. He hears something that was in the past, with someone begging him for help. So how does he go about dealing with it—with going into the past? It would a horror story set in some sort of 1930's motor court, with all the historical detail and atmosphere of that time. And so on and so forth, and so on and so forth . . . ! But right now I don't have the time for it; I'm [already] doing something else.

GRAHAM MASTERTON

They're all difficult [novels to write], though some appear to be less difficult than others. For me, *The Magic Cottage* was a breeze. *The Fog* wrote itself. Books like *Domain* were very, very difficult because there was so much research. *Sepulchre* was very, very difficult because it was so dark, and I had to keep myself in that mood all the time. I didn't want to enjoy myself while I was doing it. I had to remain very dark and sinister, so I could give myself no relief with humor or sheer enjoyment. The research aspects come into it as well—it's very difficult to stop your imagination from running away and just collate all those facts that you have, and make sense of them.

JAMES HERBERT

I was teaching speech and dramatics at the time at Occidental College in Los Angeles. It wasn't a job I was in love with, but it did give me a lot of experience. More importantly, it gave me the background for *Conjure Wife*, you see: I was married, I was working at a small conservative college. Transferred to the east, that gave me the background for Hempnell College in New England where I set the story. Now I had characters; I had to write about relations, but I had the faculty and the wives and all the business of jealousy between faculty husband and wives. So I got the background of *Conjure Wife* that way.

FRITZ LEIBER

The story is based on a woman I lived with, on and off, for a year. It was a very stormy relationship: she was one of those people who aren't what they appear to be at all. She was a very good-looking woman, very well-educated, very polished—and almost totally psychotic. She had incredible depressions, and was suicidal some of the time. For example, she would point out someone who looked particularly sad, and say, "He would be better off if he had the nerve to kill himself." I always meant to write about her someday, and that's where "Mother Darkness" came from. I then ran into an old friend of mine who was a social worker, and that's where the two ideas came together to make the story. I talked to five or six different social workers, and with one of them I went on her rounds. However inept the welfare system may be, I could see that these people were being helped, and that these social workers do make a difference in their lives. The section of the city where I live is layered very oddly. I live kind of in the middle "layer." About eight blocks from here is a fairly big ghetto, and on the top layer are all these splashy, half million dollar homes. But that ghetto is an area which I drive through almost every day. I came from a very lower class environment, and I grew up with a lot of poor black kids. So I'm optimistic about the system, but when I brought my old girlfriend into the story as Alison, it became very dark.

All fiction is speculating on life experiences, and that's all this is.

ED GORMAN

We were taking a tour of the Howe Caverns [in New York]. And the tour guide told us about the other end of the cave, which hadn't been developed, and was unlighted. He made some joke about, "If we get stuck down here, I'm the guy with the flashlight!" I thought, "My, God! I've got to write a book about this!" So I did. It's called *Midnight's Lair*, and the whole story occurs over the period of one day. Less than a day, actually. It's about a tour group that gets stuck down there—and what's on the other side of the wall at the far side of the main cavern.

RICHARD LAYMON

There was a novel called *Intruder*, and I wrote it after *The Totem*. It's a book about spouse abuse. I wanted to do a book that dramatized the horror of what it was like for a wife to be stalked by an abusive husband. What began to occur to me was that most novelists dealt with this theme realistically, in sociological ways. But what I wanted to do was write it as a horror novel. The husband, whose name was Harry, just became an implacable force of evil. He had been in a fire, which had disfigured his face, and hence he took to wearing disguises. So this poor woman, while she was on the run, never knew when this man was going to appear, or what he was going to look like! At one point in the narrative, he went to a plastic surgeon who gave him a "touch-up job," so to speak. But it didn't work, and as we near the climax, pieces of his face begin to fall off!

The problem was, it may have been *too* strong. I went to my agent and a number of publishers, and they were just aghast that I had written this. They thought this guy was *so* grotesque, he might as well have been from the moon. People *really* had trouble trying to understand what I was trying to do. As a sidebar, someone who is in the publishing business—and I hasten to add it's nobody I was ever associated with—read the book in manuscript and actually said that the woman deserved to be beaten. I don't know what this guy did at home, but his reaction scared *me* a lot.

DAVID MORRELL

I always start with the *idea*, and then fill the book with characters who will serve that idea. There are characters who come alive suddenly—every now and then someone who was a minor character in the outline will blossom into a much larger role. But generally speaking, my books generate from the idea.

JOHN SAUL

I had written half a dozen novels which were not occult. I don't even want to talk about them—now they don't seem very good at all. But they were not occult, and I was getting tired of not selling. I went to see *Barry Lyndon*, the film, which was terrible. But before it, they had a trailer for *The Omen* (which is the only thing I ever saw about *The Omen*). In it, the child was called Damien. And I had just seen *The Exorcist*, and in it the child was called Regan. So I thought, isn't that convenient, that demonic children have such interesting names. And so I thought, what if you have a demonic child named . . . Fred! I was going to do a screenplay about a demonic child named Fred. I worked on it awhile, and it turned into *The Amulet*. Fred drops out. For practice, I decided to novelize the screenplay. And the "novelization" sold—immediately! And I thought, "Well, I've done something right!" That was how I came into it, sort of back door and accidental.

MICHAEL MCDOWELL

My wife died in 1969, and I moved up from Los Angeles to San Francisco then. Not only my wife, but my mother died at that time—outliving my father by more than twenty years. So by the time I was writing *Our Lady of Darkness* I was living alone again, which I think gives a certain lonely background to the story that was more like my earliest horror writing. Where I was capitalizing on the fact that I knew how to write about a lonely individual, and so I got back to some of the feelings of those early days.

I still prefer to a write a story where the horror itself is the central theme, rather than the problems of the hero. But I did give him similar problems: I made him a recently reformed alcoholic who had lost his wife to a brain tumor. . . . The wife of a horror writer I know died that way, which was altogether a pretty ghastly business.

FRITZ LEIBER

At Bloomingdale's, on the escalator, there were a couple of nuns in their habits. And one of the nun's habits actually got caught in the thing. In real life, what happens is that there's little do-hickey that halts the apparatus. But I quickly whipped out my little notebook and jotted the incident down. It later appeared in *Playboy*—the one where the people are being *ground* in to the escalator. It was something that was simply too good not to use [later as a cartoon].

GAHAN WILSON

With most of my books some research is involved. But with *The Girl Next Door*, I knew *everything*. I just *remembered* it. So it was the easiest book to write from that perspective, but from a moral perspective it was the hardest. That is, it was a difficult technical problem for me. It was difficult because if you're writing a first-person viewpoint novel, you have to somehow deflect the reader's interest regarding the survival of whomever's narrating the story.

You're not worried if my narrator's going to live; you know he's going to live because he's telling the story thirty years later. So what you as a reader have to worry about is what *he* worries about. Finally, what he worries about a lot is what he's doing—or not doing—for the girl next door.

JACK KETCHUM

Writing to me is kind of like acting; you take on the guise of a character, and you keep in that mind-set the whole way through the work. . . . And when you write like that, and you're relaxed, it does tend to flow a lot more smoothly than it might otherwise.

Once I had the basic plot [for "Confessions of St. James"] in my head, I wrote down a list of things I was going to have to do some research on. I went down to my library to get a few things on inter-library loan. So I turned in my list, and the librarian saw that I wanted books on: cremation, curing and drying meat, and careers in the ministry. So she looked at me and said, "This is going to be a *strange* one, isn't it?" As I said before, trying to get into the character is almost like method acting. I didn't work a day on this story without having a piece of jerky by my side. And I mean the real good jerky you get from a butcher shop, not those in the thin plastic containers. So when it came to these scenes, I would tear off a piece of jerky and let it just sit in my mouth. And I think that was a big influence on my work.

CHET WILLIAMSON

It was very spontaneous. There was no plan at all. I was sitting at the typewriter and just thought I wanted to try it. I wrote very spontaneously in those days—with no plan to as to even what word was going to come next. At first, *Interview With The Vampire* was a short story. I put it away, then took it out, rewrote it, put away, took it out; rewrote it. Again and again. It was during one of these rewrites that I got ferociously involved with it, and it grew into this very weird novel. There were a number of false turns—at one point I threw out half of it and started over. But in general it was a great deal of experimenting and throwing stuff into the pot as if you were making soup.

You know, I was not a person who was obsessed with vampires, or who had pictures of them around the house. I hadn't seen any vampire movies in recent years, so it didn't grow out of any active obsession with them. It just happened that when I started to write through that image, everything came together for me. I was suddenly able to talk about reality by using fantasy. So, it opened a door. In some ways, that's what it all is for me—just the opening of one door after another.

ANNE RICE

I keep a dream diary, though it's not just for dreams. It's one kind of internal reporting. But I also write down notes as you would when you feel particularly happy, or how you feel when you feel particularly bad after some loss or some sense of disappointment. I'm constantly making notes about my own mental processes as starting places for other projects. I'll just file those away, and I have boxes and boxes of notes filled with snatches of poetry and snatches of self-analysis, if you like. Which may or may not find their way into a piece of prose, many years down the line.

I've had a few dreams which have left me uneasy in the negative sense, but there are also dreams of unease which are hugely inspiring. Inevitably, one dreams about the loss of something, such as a loved one, and I suppose that comes close to the nightmare. But I don't wake up terrified that my body is being ripped up by one of my own creatures. I'm very aware of the relationship I have with my imagination, both consciously and unconsciously. I think that my prime obsession has been the honing and sophisticating and the employing of my imagination. It's obviously the chief tool of my craft. It's also a major place for self-explanation, the means by which I understand myself best.

CLIVE BARKER

I had a dream about two characters which essentially were the Monk and a vampire. I guess I've always been more interested in the bad guys than the good guys. Instead of the usual good versus evil conflict, I thought it would be more interesting to have two fairly rotten people jockeying for position. Using it as a way to try and decide which sort of evil was actually more of a menace; usually the vampire is set up as a boogeyman character and this is source of all of our problems. Whereas I feel that even if there were such creatures—or whatever sort of aberrant social behavior we have such as Jack the Ripper or Charles Manson—as awful as they may be, they really don't cause as much trouble as the socially acceptable, institutionalized forms of cruelty, evil, and intolerance.

LES DANIELS

Much of my work contains images or details that come from dreams. I even had the peculiar experience of dreaming the typewritten manuscript in two or three cases—I saw the entire story already written out in my dream! Examples include "Time Killer" and "The Night of the Eye," which I saw typed out for me in my dream in manuscript form. I find that fascinating.

In fact, I must tell you that my novel *Darkside* originated with a dream I had one night a few years ago in which I dreamed of a Stephen King novel that doesn't really exist; it's never been written. But I dreamed I was involved in a certain kind of suburban paranoia. And I thought to myself as I was dreaming, "If I could just get this all down, it would be a great novel!" As it turned out, it had little to do with that unwritten King novel, though the aspects of a new family in a well-to-do suburban setting being menaced by teenagers comes directly from that dream.

God only knows where this all comes from! Maybe Plato was right. Or Phil Dick, who toyed with the idea that time is running backwards and that all this has happened before.

DENNIS ETCHISON

Small mid-western towns are my roots. Both of my parents were born in towns very much like Danziger. I did use a lot of my memories, and I have been back to the area where I grew up. In a lot of my books, I use a small mid-western town in some way or the other. I really like these kinds of communities—not that they all have problems like Danziger!—but I don't think I could live in one for more than a couple of weeks without going crazy. I could also say that the key idea to "Damntown" is that I sometimes write about the flip-side of a situation. Like the flip-side to "Brigadoon" which is about a town that's frozen in time. And when it comes back, it's such a lovely place that everyone is happy and wants to stay there. I thought, "What if a town was frozen in time, and then came back to the present. Only it wasn't such a nice place, and it would be hell to get out of there . . . "

GARY BRANDNER

I got the idea when I went with my family and some friends to Death Valley, and we went to this ghost town. We were wandering through this building, which seemed to have been abandoned fairly recently, judging by the pictures on the wall. We had wandered out back, which was pretty much like a junkyard. Then our wives found something, and began yelling, "Come here! Get here quick!" I figured at first someone had tripped or gotten hurt. But actually they had found a skeleton in one of the rooms that we had earlier overlooked. It was in a black coffin with a glass lid. It had a whiskey bottle resting on its shoulder, which I imagine was somebody's idea of a joke. So I figured when we got back that I just had to write a story about people coming across a skeleton, and "Wishbone" come out of that.

RICHARD LAYMON

How [Seven Steps to Midnight] came about was that in 1981, my wife and I, and [my son] Richard and his girlfriend at the time, went to Europe. We went to London, Paris, Rome, and Switzerland. And at the time I thought, "Well, I'm never going to have this kind of background again, so I'm going to start collecting booklets and taking photographs, and keeping notes, just in case I can do a novel from this." So when we got home, I tore off about a couple of hundred pages on the typewriter in a very short period of time, and then put it aside until last year. At which time I thought, "Well, maybe I better finish this now." And that's what it is: just a simple suspense story about a man being pursued, with everyone trying to get him, and what happens afterwards.

RICHARD MATHESON

There's a thriving business here in "she-males": men who are planning to go through a sex-change operation to become women. They're in the pre-op stage, and a lot of them are in the prostitute business to make enough money to pay for the operation. There's quite a few of them in the porn industry as well. And I just happen to live in a neighborhood that has a few. I thought of updating the Norman Bates idea in *Psycho* to the Nineties. But nowadays, Norman could probably do a lot better in terms of fully realizing his psychoses instead of just putting on a dress and a wig! There's a thriving drag queen scene out here in some of the nightclubs, too. Anyway, I've found there's just a lot of gender-bending in New York, and "Such a Good Baby" simply takes it to the ultimate-ultimate. The story came about not only by being surrounded by all these "she-males," but the genuine basis comes from Monty Python's *The Life of Brian.* Remember? That's where Eric Idle wants to become a woman—he wants to be called Rebecca! He even wants to have a child, and the others ask him, "What are you going to do—keep it in a shoebox?"

NANCY A. COLLINS

Like all of the Lakeside Stories, "The Marble Boy" is vaguely autobiographical, although this one is more autobiographical than most because there *was* a graveyard just like the one described. And it was part of a kid's tradition where I grew up to sneak into it and wander around. There actually was a marble boy—a little statue like that; it was a particularly spooky graveyard. But it was a great place in my childhood, and I loved it.

As I said in the story, they're forever fascinating to kids because they're this weird hole in this whole fabric that grown-ups have tried to construct. Cemeteries are all about *doom*, and it's a horrendous denial of our mortality. They're very scary to kids because, with

everything grown-ups are saying about life, there's this big, fat, scary piece of doubt right in the middle of everything.
GAHAN WILSON

I can remember the first idea that came to me, that began to grow and mutate into what eventually gelled into "Kirby." I was driving along, reflecting on my childhood, as we all do. And I was thinking how, as adults, we don't have the fantasy playmates that we did as children. That was the starting point. The next step out was to ask myself, "What if some little kid could bring his fantasy a little closer to reality?" Because when we're involved with these fantasy games as children, we're able to suspend our disbelief a lot more than we ever will be able to again in our lives.
JOSEPH A. CITRO

[In creating "Mop Up"] I had a vision of a young, scared soldier in the ruins of a city, who, with a few buddies, were getting their asses ripped by these vile creatures in this post-apocalyptic world, and then meet this nice young lady survivor somewhere along the way. I thought of the general situation a long time ago, but couldn't figure out how to make a novel out of it. Then I realized this [anthology] would be my opportunity to flesh it out [as a novella]. It took me about three weeks to do it. It was inspired in part by George Romero's movies—*Night of the Living Dead*. *The Crazies*. And I think maybe a little of John Carpenter's *Assault on Precinct 13*, and some of the movies that have been spawned by Richard Matheson's *I Am Legend*.
RICHARD LAYMON

I was playing golf with Jerry Sohl, who's a science fiction writer who was quite well-known some years ago, and when we were coming in for lunch from the course, people were running about saying that John Kennedy had just been shot. And we went in for lunch, and everybody was talking about it, and we were so distressed we just couldn't think of going back and playing again. So we were driving home through the San Fernando Valley, when a truck began tailgating us through this narrow pass. And *really* tailgating us—to a point where Jerry had to speed up and pull over to the side of the road, spinning around and raising dust and everything. And on top of Kennedy's assassination, to have this happen, we were like screaming out the window at this guy!

But then, being a true writer, as soon as the car came to a halt and the dust came down, I borrowed an envelope off of him and wrote down the story idea. And ten years later, I wrote it as *Duel.*

RICHARD MATHESON

I've just always thought that the garbage disposal was a very frightening concept. And it's always been in the back of my mind that there's something *down* there. Because we can never *see* what's down there. [To conceive "Disposal"] what I did was to lean back in my chair, and look up at the ceiling, and think about what might be down there. And what might come up out of there. And who might be most frightened by something coming out of a disposal? It's just the old "what if?" game.

GARY BRANDNER

Right before attending the most recent World Fantasy Convention, I had a dream about the first World Fantasy Convention that I attended. At the time I was not even remotely well-known, and so I was very thrilled with a fan came to me at a party and asked for my signature. I'm pretty sure that I dreamed there were a long line of autograph seekers, stretching out to infinity . . . ! But in this nightmare—it started out as a nice dream and turned into a nightmare—this young fan then dogged my every step, phoned me at all hours, and begin to drop in at my home unannounced. . . . And in true nightmare fashion, I was beginning to suspect, with a certain frightening anticipation, that this fan was closing in on me for whatever hideous reason my dream/nightmare did not explain. So when I woke up, I decided one way to find out the reasons would be to write a story around my dream/nightmare: "God's Mouth to your Ear."

J.N. WILLIAMSON

The inspiration for "Making Belinda" came when my wife and I visited the south coast of England, when our first son was very small. And as she lay in the sand sunbathing, I made a replica of her out of sand right next to her. It occurred to me that this was a very bizarre but interesting thought if you could just make as many willing women as you wanted to just out of sand. . . . The idea returned to me last year when I went to Jersey, and stayed at the very hotel that's mentioned in the story. I saw how the kids on the beach were making little creatures and castles out of sand, and the bizarre idea returned to me to have the sand replicas come to life.

I very much value short story writing for the practice and the training it gives me. One thing I'm always striving for is the believability factor. You've got to work on the time and the place you create to make it believable. I work very hard on the background, not to be a slave to detail, but to bring out the essence of the reality of the situation. It's important to me, in this story, to try and get across what the seaside at Jersey is truly like. That's just as important as getting across what it's like to make a woman out of sand come to life at the beach. You have to make them work together to create the illusion.

To make simple reality believable is really the hardest trick of all.

GRAHAM MASTERTON

I wrote "Perfect Days" in four days, and revised it the following week. I had been carrying the story around in my head for so long that when I sat down to write it, it came out very easily. No angst. The angst comes in the sixteen hours a day that I'm not sitting at my desk. Generally the stories flow out so easily because I've spent so much time preparing and plotting them in my head. I never sit down with just a rough idea and start to write; I can't work like that. I outline the story really heavily, and I know precisely where I'm going with the story, and what I want the story to do before I sit down to write it. Every word counts in a short story, and as a result you can't afford to ramble and experiment and go down garden paths the way you sometimes can in a novel. A short story is like a poem in that every word has to count, and every sentence has to add to the whole.

Two ideas led me to write "Perfect Days." I live near the national retirement home for the Brotherhood of Masons. And it's really beautiful out there, it's like a giant English country estate that goes on for acres and acres. My wife and I went out there on Christmas Eve, and it was just a really beautiful day. And I thought, "If you were an old person waiting for death in this place, what a *wonderful* day this would be to die!' So I held that idea for years before another idea came to me more recently. And that was the idea of a serial killer who was never caught. What happens when serial killers grow old? Do they still have the those passions that inspired them when they were young? Or do they dull, like other passions dull with age? Then the two ideas finally clicked together and I thought, "Ah! Now here's the story!" I can examine the feelings that a person like this would have, and give him one, final, perfect day.

CHET WILLIAMSON

"I'm Not A Criminal" really happened—or at least a lot that was very close enough to what I put in the story. I had actually bought a new car—a Jeep Cherokee—and I took my family for a three week driving trip. And while we were driving through the Redwood forests of northern California, we saw this hitchhiker. And he was actually carrying this cardboard sign that said, "I'm not a criminal." A lot of the dialogue in the story came from my wife and I discussing that incident. We had a ball talking about this guy and his sign. I knew right then that I *had* to write a story about it. (And I actually *did* drive through the Redwood mentioned in the story—I didn't chicken out!) So after we had this long discussion of who would be crazy enough to pick up this guy, we drove on and stopped at a restaurant. We ate there, left, and drove some distance, and then we came upon this guy again! Just like in the story! So *somebody* had believed him, and apparently given him a ride. Unless he had already killed them, and stolen their car and it had already broken down. . . . So maybe his sign was true, but there was *no* way we were going to pick him up. I wanted to write a story about this guy, but I figured one of us didn't have to end up in a shallow grave to get all the details right.

RICHARD LAYMON

The idea for "The Little Green Ones" originally came to me when I was in London, attending the 1988 World Fantasy Convention. The fact of the matter is, just like this poor guy, I found myself lost in a cemetery. I was suffering from jet-lag, and because I work from dusk to dawn, the degree of jet-lag there was even worse. And I found myself wandering through this huge cemetery in London which was located somewhere between my hotel and the convention hotel. I had walked past this strange old Victorian cemetery a dozen times before. I don't even know why I went in; in spite of being a horror writer, I *don't* frequent cemeteries for entertainment. I remember it seemed quite large—I never explored the whole site. But shortly after I wandered in, I came upon the tomb that I refer to in the story, and standing next to it were these statues of these little green kids. They are real, just as the cemetery as described in the story is real. And I was really taken aback by these strange, life-size statues of these little kids. As I said, with the jet-lag I felt in a weakened state of mind, and they just really got to me. And I did in fact have nightmares about them while I was in London. I don't know if others were being directed here by some local guide on the idea that this cemetery was an interesting place to visit, but I was drawn back to it several times, and found other horror writers from the convention were also haunting this place. Including Charles L. Grant and Chet Williamson, who took pictures of the little children.

Amazingly, a lot of the strange details in the story also really occurred. For example, the green motif running through the story—on the last day of the convention, for the banquet, every course they served was colored green! I even remember a woman at the banquet who wore green contact lenses. . . . But I wanted to write this story from the first time I saw the green children. This is the only one I've ever written based on a personal experience of something that really, really disturbed me, that really haunted me. So I just *had* to write it.
LES DANIELS

I did "Breakfast at Earl's" in two days, pretty much from 9:30 a.m. to 3:00 p.m. each day. By the end of that second day, I had what I thought was my first finished draft—which is not anywhere near the final—but it's the first showable draft. Because that's the important thing for me, whether it's short stories or novels: you just gotta start and then blast through until you reach the end. Then you pick up the mess you made afterwards! It was just about this time last year, and I was driving down towards a shopping mall and I saw where some organization had what they called a "shopper's breakfast." And right away that made me flash me onto a "hunter's breakfast." This is a pretty traditional thing up in Maine, and I would assume elsewhere where hunting is an annual event. Now I'm not an avid anti-hunting activist, but I don't see a whole lot of reasons for people in our society today to hunt, unless it is for actually needing the meat to survive. So "Hunter's Breakfast" was the original title, and suggested the original take-off point for the setting: a group of hunters eating breakfast in a small town cafe or restaurant before going out on their hunt. "I changed the title when I considered that the story was going to see first publication in a horror anthology, and I didn't want to insult the reader's intelligence by pretending they couldn't see through that title right away. The challenge was to create a situation where the reader and one of the characters in the story knew what was going on, while

the other characters didn't. The fun of the story for me was the dramatic irony that we know what they're eating, and they don't.
RICK HAUTALA

"The Chill" was written after I saw a pair of tennis shoes sitting on the sidewalk, a policeman directing traffic, and a crowd gathering around. I then noticed that there was a huge dent in this car parked at the curb, and then I saw there was a canvas thrown over a body in the gutter. Then somebody told me that a man had jumped off the top of the building—had hit the street to hard that it knocked him out of his tennis shoes—and then the body had bounced on top of the car. The fact that that building was adjacent to a health food store, where I was headed to have lunch, was particularly provocative. The juxtaposition of life and death in that one building . . . !

But just as many stories come out of my dreams, or an experience of looking out a window at something. It's all part of my memory. Usually I see the entire story flash in front of me in the space of a few seconds. I never know when it's going to happen. But I've trained myself to recognize and hold onto those moments. It may take years to explore that "flash" and nail it to the page in its most perfect form.
DENNIS ETCHISON

For *Rosemary's Baby*, basically I started with the idea of a woman being pregnant with something that the reader knew was not what she was expecting. Where I came to that from was from the movie *King Kong*, where the first third is really the best, because you haven't seen Kong yet—it's just the anticipation. And I thought, "Gee, if the woman's pregnant, whatever it is that's inside her, it should be really spooky." And then I thought, "Well, what could it be?" And the first thing I thought of was something from outer space. But John Wyndham had done that already with *The Midwich Cuckoos*. So I realized if it couldn't be from outer space, it's got to be the child of Satan.

But I knew I had to make it very realistic—as realistic as possible. Which is why the book is filled with actual news events of the day. Which for a time, subsequently, seemed like a mistake, because it dates the book with the very specific events mentioned. But I hope not; I hope it still holds up.
IRA LEVIN

I came up with the idea for the "Madman" long before there ever was a story [called "Madman Stan"]. As I recall, my daughter Kelly left the front door unlocked one night. And to break her of the habit, I told her there was a guy who wandered the neighborhood at night, trying all the doors, looking for one that wasn't locked. While I was making that up, it occurred to me that it even scared *me*. Months later, she had a friend staying over for the night, and I told them both the story. The girl started crying, and then called up her mother to have her take her home! When it came time to make it into a story, I thought up the angle of the babysitter telling the tale to give it a structure. I did have some trouble giving the madman a name. I remembered a movie called *Madman* where a guy told a spooky story around a campfire. But in early drafts I called the character "Madman Marz" after the character in the movie. Then I simply called him "Madman." [I finally settled on] Stan because it's such a nice name for someone who's a total lunatic.

RICHARD LAYMON

REFERENCE SECTION

A Reader's Guide to Writing Horror

For those new in their exploration of contemporary horror and dark suspense, an examination of any of the following texts and periodicals (plus an investigation of certain web sites on the Internet) should begin to bring one up to speed.

Incidentally, if there appear to be more studies listed about Stephen King than any other writer in the reference section, be advised that (at last count) there are reportedly some thirty published books about the man who just happens to be the world's bestselling author. There are also enough critical studies of Anne Rice and Clive Barker as to constitute a cottage industry (dissecting King has become more like a multi-national conglomerate) in analyzing their every word and creative endeavor. (Indeed, by the time this present volume is out, there should be a major new biography of Barker by acclaimed critic Douglas E. Winter, as well as a major new biography of Koontz by popular critic Katherine Ramsland.)

Periodicals:

Necrofile: The Review of Horror Fiction
Necronomicon Press
P.O. Box 1304,
Warwick, RI 02893
(web site address: www.necropress.com)

The critical guide to all things worth mentioning and admiring in contemporary horror fiction. Currently available only by subscription. Includes a regular column by Ramsey Campbell.

Beyond their state-of-the-art criticism, "Necrofile" is the only publication which regularly lists every major book newly published—both here and in England—dealing with the genre. In both fiction *and* non-fiction. Wonderfully exhaustive.

Cemetery Dance
P.O. Box 943
Abingdon, MD 21009

The premier newsstand publication devoted to the latest fiction, non-fiction, and reviews of the horror and dark suspense field. Every major writer working today has appeared here at some point, including the best of the new talents. Meticulously edited by Richard T. Chizmar (who is also making his name known as a writer of fiction) "Cemetery Dance" features as well a wealth of insightful columns, commentary, and reviews.

Worlds of Fantasy & Horror
123 Crooked Lane,
King of Prussia, PA 19406-2570

Edited by the infatigable Darrell Schweitzer (also a well-known critic, scholar, short story writer, and author), the publication is currently the only other newsstand publication devoted to the genre. Formerly "Weird Tales," the magazine continues to publish stories in the tradition of classic horror, both supernatural and psychological in nature. Also publishes interviews and book reviews.

Hellnotes
27780 Donkey Mine Road,
Oak Run, CA 96069
(web site address: www.horrornet.com/hellnote.htm)

A *weekly* trade newsletter (available in on-line, fax, and hardcopy subscriptions) covering horror in the media, with an editorial slant for the professional writer. "Hell Notes" also runs brief interviews and book reviews, and is edited by David B. Silva and Paul F. Olson, two of the field's most experienced editors.

Phantasmagoria: the Stephen King Newsletter
P.O. Box 3602,
Williamsburg, VA 23187

Presently the only regularly published newsletter devoted to all things Stephen King. Published and edited by George Beahm, one of the world's leading authorities on King, the amount of material which appears in successive issues is fast evolving this already comprehensive publication into a full-fledged magazine.

Fangoria
475 Park Avenue South,
New York, N.Y. 10016

America's reigning newsstand periodical devoted to horror in the mass media, primarily motion pictures and television. Some coverage, however, is regularly given to horror authors.

The Dark Side
P.O. Box 36,
Liskeard, Cornwall PL14 4YT
England
(web site address: http://80.compuserve.com/homepages/stray_cat/d arkside.htm)

England's reigning newsstand periodical devoted to horror in the mass media, primarily motion pictures and television. Some coverage, however, is regularly given to horror authors.

Organizations:

Horror Writers Association
P.O. Box 50577
Palo Alto, CA 94303
(web site address: www.horror.org)

The first and only international organization for horror writers, critics, scholars, agents, and other professionals associated with the field. The organization originated in 1984 as "HOWL" (Horror Occult Writers League), the brainchild of Robert R. McCammon. (A history of the organization, written by the present author, is included in the critical anthology *Writing Horror: A Handbook by the Horror Writers Association*, edited by Mort Castle.) It goes without saying that anyone who has any interest whatsoever in horror literature should be a member of this organization, which includes amongst its roster Ray Bradbury, Stephen King, and Richard Matheson.

Horror on the Internet:

Basically, selective use of results generated by using the keywords "Horror Literature" or "Horror Authors" should be enough to open the appropriate Pandora's Box of darkly pleasant surprises. As one might imagine, just about anything you could ever want to know about the genre, your favorite author, how to find a local writer's group, or the latest catalog of your favorite rare book dealer (such as "The Overlook Connection" and "DreamHaven Books" to name only two of the best) may be found here.

Although they may conceivably change without notice, here are the current URL addresses of several mega-web sites; reach these to start your journey into the "dark side of the web." (Already taken, by the way, as a great web site: www.cascade.net/darkweb.html)

- HORRORNET (www. horrornet.com)
- DARK ECHO'S HORROR WEB (www.darkecho.com)
- THE CABINET OF DR. CASEY
(www.cat.pdx.edu-caseyh/horror/index.html)
- HORROR AT ARNZEN'S ARBOR VITAE
(http://darkwing.uoregon.edu/-mikea/horror.html)
- THE NIGHT GALLERY (www.wbm.ca/users/kgreggai/indexa.html)
- FIONA'S FEAR AND LOATHING (www.oceanstar.com/horror/

Incidentally, many popular authors have numerous "official" or fan-maintained web sites. Stephen King, Dean Koontz, Anne Rice, Clive Barker, Peter Straub, Robert R. McCammon, Poppy Z. Brite, and Neil Gaiman are only a few of those thus well represented in the endless abyss of cyberspace. In actuality, virtually every author included in this present volume has either a web site or an e-mail address. The Horror Writers Association maintains a listing of authors (only members, however) who have web sites or e-mail addresses, with more comprehensive listings to be unearthed at Mike Arnzen's "Arbor Vitae" and the HorrorNet.

Selected Reference Books:

Ashley, Michael. *Who's Who in Horror and Fantasy Fiction*. New York: Taplinger, 1977.

Bail, Paul. *John Saul: A Critical Companion*. Westport: Greenwood Press, 1996.

Beahm, George (editor). *The Stephen King Companion*. Kansas City: Andrews and McMeel, 1989.

_____. *The Stephen King Story*. Kansas City: Andrews and McMeel, 1991.

_____ (editor). *The Unauthorized Anne Rice Companion*. Kansas City: Andrews and McMeel, 1996.

Bleiler, Everett F. *The Guide to Supernatural Fiction*. Kent, OH: Kent State University Press, 1983.

Bloch, Robert. *Once Around the Bloch: An Unauthorized Autobiography*. New York, Tor Books. 1993.

Blue, Tyson. *Observations from the Terminator*. San Bernardino, CA: The Borgo Press, 1997.

Campbell, Ramsey (with Stefan Dziemianowicz & S.T. Joshi). The *Core of Ramsey Campbell: A Bibliography & Reader's Guide*. West Warwick, R.I.: Necronomicon Press, 1995.

Castle, Mort (editor). *The Horror Writers Association: Writing Horror*. Cincinnati, OH: Writer's Digest Books, 1997.

Clarke, Boden and Hopkins, James (editors). *The Work of William F. Nolan: An Annotated Bibliography and Guide*. San Bernardino, CA: The Borgo Press, 1988.

Collings, Michael. *The Work of Stephen King: An Annotated Bibliography and Guide*. San Bernardino, CA: The Borgo Press, 1996.

Crawford, Gary William. *Ramsey Campbell*. Mercer Island, WA: Starmont House, 1988.

D'Ammassa, Don. *D'Ammassa's Guide to Modern Horror Fiction*. San Bernardino, CA: The Borgo Press, 1997.

Engel, Joel. Rod Serling: *The Dreams and Nightmares of Life in the Twilight Zone*. Chicago, IL: Contemporary Books, 1989.

Golden, Christopher (editor). *Cut! Horror Writers on Horror Film*. New York: Berkley Books, 1992.

Greenberg, Martin H., Gorman, Ed, and Munster, Bill (editors).*The Dean Koontz Companion*. New York: Berkley, 1994.

Johnson, Wayne L. *Ray Bradbury*. ("Recognition" series.) New York: Frederick Ungar, 1980.

Jones, Stephen, and Newman, Kim (editors). *Horror: 100 Best Books*. New York: Carroll & Graf, 1988.

Jones, Stephen (editor). *Clive Barker's Shadows In Eden*. Lancaster, PA: Underwood-Miller, 1991.

_____ (editor). *James Herbert: By Horror Haunted*. London: New English Library, 1992.

Kies, Cosette N. *Presenting Young Adult Horror Fiction*. New York: Twayne Publishers, 1992.

King, Stephen *Danse Macabre*. New York: Everest House, 1981.

Klein, T.E.D. *Raising Goosebumps for Fun and Profit*. New York: Footsteps Press, 1988.

Larson, Randall D. (editor). *The Complete Robert Bloch: An Illustrated, International Bibliography*. Sunnyvale, CA: Fandom Unlimited Enterprises, 1986.

_____ *Robert Bloch: A Reader's Guide*. Mercer Island, WA: Starmont House, 1986.

_____ (editor). *The Robert Bloch Companion: Collected Interviews– 1969-1989*. Mercer Island, WA: Starmont Books, 1989.

Matheson, Richard, and Mainhardt, Ricia (editors). *Robert Bloch: Appreciations of the Master*. New York: Tor Books, 1995.

Munster, Bill (editor). *Sudden Fear: The Horror and Dark Suspense Fiction of Dean Koontz*. Mercer Island, WA: Starmont House, 1988.

Nolan, William F. *The Ray Bradbury Companion*. Detroit, MI: Gale Research, 1975.

_____ *How to Write Horror Fiction*. Cincinnati, OH: Writer's Digest Books, 1990.

Olander, Joseph D. and Greenberg, Martin H. (editors). *Ray Bradbury*. ("Writers of the 21st Century" series.) New York: Taplinger, 1980.

Proulx, Kevin. *Fear to the World: 11 Voices in a Chorus of Fear*. Mercer Island, WA: Starmont House, 1992.

Ramsland, Katherine. *Prism of the Night: An Anne Rice Biography*. New York: Dutton, 1991.

Rathbun, Mark and Flanagan, Graeme. *Richard Matheson: He Is Legend. An Illustrated Bio-bibliography*. Chico, CA: Privately Published, 1984.

Riley, Michael. *Conversations with Anne Rice*. New York. Fawcett Books, 1996.

Schweitzer, Darrell (editor). *Discovering Modern Horror Fiction I*. Mercer Island, WA: Starmont House, 1985.

_____ (editor). *Discovering Modern Horror Fiction II*. Mercer Island, WA: Starmont House, 1988.

_____ . *Speaking of Horror: Interviews with Writers of the Supernatural*. San Bernardino, CA: The Borgo Press, 1994.

Spignesi, Stephen J. *The Complete Stephen King Encyclopedia*.Chicago, IL: Contemporary Books, 1991.

Staicar, Tom. *Friz Leiber*. ("Recognition" series.) New York: Frederick Ungar, 1983.

Stine, R.L. *It Came From Ohio: My Life as a Writer*. New York: Scholastic Books, 1997.

Sullivan, Jack (editor). *The Penquin Encyclopedia of Horror and the Supernatural*. New York: Viking Penguin, 1986.

Tymn, Marshall B. (editor). *Horror Literature: A Core Collection and Reference Guide*. New York: Bowker, 1981.

Underwood, Tim and Miller, Chuck. (editors). *Bare Bones: Conversations on Terror with Stephen King*. New York: McGraw-Hill, 1988.

_____. (editors). *Feast of Fear: Conversations with Stephen King.* New York: Caroll & Graf, 1989.

Wiater, Stanley. *Dark Dreamers: Conversations with the Masters of Horror.* New York: Avon Books, 1990.

_____. *Dark Visions: Conversations with the Masters of the Horror Film.* New York: Avon Books, 1992.

Williamson, J.N. (editor). *How to Write Tales of Horror, Fantasy & Science Fiction.* Cincinnati, OH: Writer's Digest Books, 1987.

Winter, Douglas E. *Stephen King: The Art of Darkness.* New York.New American Library, 1984.

_____ *Faces of Fear: Encounters with the Creators of Modern Horror.* New York; Berkley Books, 1985.

Wolf, Leonard. *Horror: A Connoisseur's Guide to Literature and Film.* New York: Facts on File, 1989.

Wood, Martin, and Clarke, Boden. *The Work of Gary Brandner: An Annotated Bibliography and Guide.* San Bernandino, CA: The Borgo Press, 1995.

Modern Horror Fiction:
A Selection of 113 Best Books

Although it's nearly impossible to judge an author on the basis of a single work, the fact remains that any new reader must nevertheless begin their exploration of this, or any genre, one title at a time. While the total of one hundred and thirteen seemed undeniably appropriate to a list of these modern works, regardless of whether the title had been originally marketed to the general public as "Horror" or "Dark Fantasy" or "Dark Suspense."

Admittedly it would have been a simple enough task to just recommend ten popular works by Stephen King, eight by Dean Koontz, five by Clive Barker, and so on, by merely following the mainstream bestseller lists.

Yet this would only have lead to the undesired exclusion of those less known—and yet no less highly skilled—practitioners of the art of literary terror. While the entire spectrum of the colors of darkness must be touched upon, with styles ranging from the most repulsively explicit to the most maddeningly subtle. Rest assured, even though you may not have heard of all of these authors, each and every one has received critical success or awards in his or her career.

Even so, where there has been a choice between a novel and a short story collection, I have almost always deferred to the collection to better serve as a "sampler" of that author's talents. As the reader can no doubt appreciate by now, the most difficult format for any writer to find success is in the short story, where every single word is absolutely crucial to the final, unavoidable, couldn't be any other way, conclusion.

And by the term "modern," this particular time-frame refers to books either written (with the exceptions of retrospective collections by such past masters as Beaumont, Bloch, Cave, Dahl, Long, Wellman, and seminal works by Bradbury and Jackson) or published since 1960.

I am indebted to noted author and critic Douglas E. Winter, who composed a similar listing of at least equal value in his own invaluable *Faces of Fear*.

1. Robert Aickman: *Tales of Love and Death* (1977)
2. Jonathan Aycliffe: *The Vanishment* (1993)
3. J.G. Ballard: *Crash* (1973)
4. Ian Banks: *The Wasp Factory* (1984)
5. Clive Barker: *The Books of Blood* (1984-1986)
6. Charles Beaumont: *The Howling Man and Other Stories* (1992)
7. Charles Birkin: *The Smell of Evil* (1964)
8. Stephen R. Bissette: *Aliens: Tribes* (1992)
9. William Peter Blatty: *The Exorcist* (1971)
10. Robert Bloch: *Selected Short Stories* (1988)
11. Michael Blumlein: *The Brains of Rats* (1990)
12. Ray Bradbury: *The October Country* (1955)
13. Gary Brandner: *The Howling* (1977)
14. Joseph Payne Brennan: *The Shapes of Midnight* (1980)
15. Poppy Z. Brite: *Swamp Foetus* (1993)
16. Ramsey Campbell: *The Face That Must Die* (1979)
17. Jonathan Carroll: *The Panic Hand* (1996)
18. Angela Carter: *Burning Your Boats: Collected Stories* (1995)
19. Hugh B. Cave: *Death Stalks the Night* (1995)
20. R. Chetwynd-Hayes: *Shudders and Shivers* (1995)
21. Joseph A. Citro: *Deux-X* (1994)
22. Alan M. Clark: *The Pain Doctors of Suture Self General* (1995)
23. Douglas Clegg: *The Children's Hour* (1996)
24. Nancy A. Collins: *Nameless Sins* (1994)
25. Matthew J. Costello: *Homecoming* (1992)
26. Peter Crowther & James Lovegrove: *Escardy Gap* (1996)
27. Roald Dahl: *Tales of the Unexpected* (1979)
28. Les Daniels: *The Black Castle* (1978)
29. David Drake: *From the Heart of Darkness* (1983)
30. Harlan Ellison: *The Essential Ellison* (1987)
31. Elizabeth Engstrom: *Lizard Wine* (9916)
32. Dennis Etchison: *The Dark Country* (1982)

33. John Farris: *Scare Tactics* (1988)
34. Neil Gaiman: *Sandman* (1988 to 1996)
35. Stephen Geller: *She Let Him Continue* (1966)
36. Ray Garton: *Methods of Madness* (1990)
37. Ed Gorman: *Moonchasers* (1996)
38. Charles L. Grant: *Tales from the Nightside* (1981)
39. Stephen Gregory: *The Cormorant* (1986)
40. Davis Grubb: *12 Stories of Suspense and the Supernatural* (1964)
41. Thomas Harris: *Red Dragon* (1981)
42. Rick Hautala: *The Mountain King* (1996)
43. James Herbert: *Portent* (1996)
44. Eric C. Higgs: *The Happy Man* (1985)
45. William Hjortsberg: *Falling Angel* (1978)
46. Brian Hodge: *The Convulsion Factory* (1996)
47. Nancy Holder: *Dead in the Water* (1994)
48. A. M. Homes: *The End of Alice* (1996)
49. Shirley Jackson: *The Haunting of Hill House* (1959)
50. George Clayton Johnson: *Twilight Zone Scripts & Stories* (1977)
51. Jack Ketchum: *The Girl Next Door* (1989)
52. Stephen King: *Skeleton Crew* (1985)
53. Russell Kirk: *The Surly Sullen Bell* (1962)
54. T.E.D. Klein: *Dark Gods* (1985)
55. Dean Koontz: *Strange Highways* (1995)
56. Kathe Koja: *Strange Angels* (1994)
57. Joe R. Lansdale: *The Nightrunners* (1987)
58. Stephen Laws: *Darkfall* (1992)
59. Richard Laymon: *Out Are The Lights* (1991)
60. Edward Lee: *Succubi* (1992)
61. Tanith Lee: *Dreams of Dark and Light* (1986)
62. Fritz Leiber: *Our Lady of Darkness* (1977)
63. Ira Levin: *Rosemary's Baby* (1967)
64. Thomas Ligotti: *The Nightmare Factory* (1996)
65. Bentley Little: *Evil Deeds* (1995)
66. Frank Belknap Long: *The Rim of the Unknown* (1972)
67. Tim Lucas: *Throat Sprockets* (1994)
68. Brian Lumley: *Fruiting Bodies and Other Fungi* (1993)
69. Robert Marasco. *Burnt Offerings* (1973)
70. Elizabeth Massie: *Shadow Dreams* (1996)
71. Graham Masterton: *Night Warriors* (1985)
72. Richard Matheson: *Collected Stories* (1989)
73. Richard Cristian Matheson: *Scars* (1987)

74. Robert R. McCammon: *Blue World* (1990)
75. Michael McDowell: *Toplin* (1985)
76. Ian McEwan: *The Cement Garden* (1978)
77. Patrick McGrath: *Blood and Water and Other Tales* (1988)
78. Stanley McNail: *Something Breathing* (1965)
79. Frank Miller: *Sin City* (1992 to present)
80. Rex Miller: *Slob* (1987)
81. Thomas F. Monteleone: *The Blood of the Lamb* (1992)
82. Alan Moore: *From Hell* (1994-96)
83. David Morrell: *Testament* (1975)
84. Kim Newman: *Anno-Dracula* (1992)
85. William F. Nolan: *Things Beyond Midnight* (1984)
86. Joyce Carol Oates: *Haunted: Tales of the Grotesque* (1994)
87. Norman Partridge: *Bad Intentions* (1996)
88. Anne Rice: *Interview with the Vampire* (1976)
89. Ray Russell: *Haunted Castles* (1985)
90. Wayne Allen Sallee: *With Wounds Still Wet* (1996)
91. John Saul: *Suffer the Children* (1977)
92. David J. Schow: *Seeing Red* (1990)
93. Lewis Shepard: *The Jaguar Hunter* (1987)
94. Dan Simmons: *Lovedeath* (1993)
95. John Skipp & Craig Spector: *Dead Lines* (1989)
96. Peter Straub: *Houses with Doors* (1990)
97. Whitley Strieber: *Evenings with Demons* (1996)
98. Theodore Sturgeon: *Some of Your Blood* (1961)
99. S.P. Somtow: *Vampire Junction* (1984)
100. Bernard Taylor: *The Reaping* (1980)
101. Lucy Taylor: *The Flesh Artist* (1994)
102. Melanie Tem: *Prodigal* (1991)
103. Thomas Tessier: *The Nightwalker* (1979)
104. Roland Topor: *The Tenant* (1964)
105. Robert Turner: *Shroud 9* (1970)
106. Thomas Tyron: *The Other* (1971)
107. Karl Edward Wagner: *In A Lonely Place* (1983)
108. Manly Wade Wellman: *Worse Things Waiting* (1978)
109. F. Paul Wilson: *Sibs* (1991)
110. Chet Williamson: *Reign* (1990)
111. J.N. Williamson: *Don't Take Away the Light* (1993)
112. T.M. Wright: *Strange Seed* (1977)
113. Chelsea Quinn Yarbo: *Signs & Portents* (1984)

The Best in Short Fiction:
Anthologies

A sampling of contemporary anthologies which hopefully comprises much of the very best of modern horror fiction.

At minimum, the new reader should obtain any and all volumes of these ongoing series: *The Year's Best Fantasy and Horror* edited by Ellen Datlow and Terri Windling; England's *Best New Horror*, edited by Stephen Jones; *Borderlands*, edited by Thomas F. Monteleone and Elizabeth Monteleone; the *Dark Destiny* series, edited by Edward E. Kramer; England's *Narrow Houses* series, edited by Peter Crowther. (The Datlow/Windling series is especially rewarding for scholars in that each volume—with the assistance of critic Ed Bryant—takes an in-depth look at the entire "Year in Horror," examining the publishing industry, awards, the small press, trends, obituaries; any and all relevant aspects of the field in popular culture.)

For those interested in the new erotic horror, seek out Jeff Gelb's always steamy and splattery *Hot Blood* series. A "classic" theme series, under the general editorship of Bryon Preiss, has unleashed several enjoyable volumes, including *The Ultimate Dracula, The Ultimate Frankenstein, The Ultimate Werewolf,* etc.

In completed series: *The Year's Best Horror Stories*, edited first by Gerald W. Page and later by Karl Edward Wagner; the *Masques* series, edited by J.N. Williamson; *Night Visions* (various editors); the *Whispers* series, edited by Stuart David Schiff; the *Masters of Darkness* edited by Dennis Etchison; the *Taboo* series edited by Stephen R.

Bissette and Nancy O'Conner; and the *Shadows* series edited by Charles L. Grant.

The Horror Writers Association has an ongoing series of original anthologies, edited (to date) by such luminaries as Robert R. McCammon, F. Paul Wilson, Ramsey Campbell, Peter Straub, and Whitley Strieber.

And Barnes & Nobles continues to publish a noteworthy series of "instant remainder" volumes which showcase the genre from a variety of aspects and themes. Many of these commendable volumes (which often showcase the short-short story) are edited by Stefan Dziemianowicz, John Gregory Bentacourt, Marvin Kaye, and Robert Weinberg, among others.

In summation, if you come across an anthology with the names of any of the above editors on the spine or cover, you can be dutifully assured of a frighteningly worthwhile experience.

RECOMMENDED NON-SERIES TITLES

As with the previously noted titles by individual authors, the following editors are listed with only one anthology (or limited series) to their credit. This is somewhat misleading, as several of the previously mentioned editors (Datlow, Crowther, Jones, Grant) have extensive and remarkable credits as editors. Indeed, Martin H. Greenberg's credits, in various genres, literally number in the several hundreds! Robert Weinberg has some 100 non-fiction titles and anthologies to his credit, with clearly no intention (you must forgive me just this once) of giving up the ghost. Few of the anthologists mentioned below (with the obvious exception of England's legendary Peter Haining) are as prolific. The title in question is therefore this author's opinion of that editor—or editors—most critically acclaimed for popular effort to date.

1. Baker, Mike. *Young Blood* (1994)
2. Bloch, Robert. *Psycho-Paths* (1991)
3. Brite, Poppy Z. *Love In Vein* (two volumes) (1994)
4. Campbell, Ramsey. *New Terrors* (two volumes) (1980)
5. Chizmar, Richard T. *The Best of Cemetery Dance* (1997)
6. Collins, Charles M. *A Feast of Blood* (1967)
7. Collins, Nancy, Kramer, Edward, and Greenberg, Martin H. Dark Love (1995)
8. Dozois, Gardner. *Killing Me Softly* (1995)
9. Freeman, Lucy. *Killers of the Mind* (1974)

10. Gorman, Ed, and Greenberg, Martin H. *Stalkers* (1989)
11. Greenberg, Martin H., Morgan, Jill M., Weinberg, Robert. *Great Writers & Kids Write Spooky Stories* (1995)
12. Haining, Peter. *The Unspeakable People* (1969)
13. Hartwell, David G. *The Dark Descent* (1987)
14. Knight, Amarantha. *Sex Macabre* (1996)
15. Lansdale, Joe, and Lansdale, Karen. *Dark At Heart* (1992)
16. Maclay, John. *Voices from the Night* (1994)
17. McCauley, Kirby. *Dark Forces* (1980)
18. Manguel, Alberto *Dark Arrows: Great Stories of Revenge* (1987)
19. Masterton, Graham. *Scare Care* (1989)
20. Nolan, William F., and Greenberg, Martin H. *Urban Horrors* (1990)
21. Olson, Paul F., and Silva, David B. *Post Mortem* (1989)
22. Pelan, John. *Darkside: Horror for the New Millenium* (1996)
23. Pronzini, Bill, Malzberg, Barry, and Greenberg, Martin H. *The Arbor House Treasury of Horror and the Supernatural* (1981)
24. Ptacek, Katherine. *Women of Darkness* (two volumes) (1988)
25. Raisor, Gary. *Obsessions* (1991)
26. Roche, Thomas S. *Noirotica* (two volumes) (1996)
27. (Russell, Ray?). The Playboy Book of Horror and the Supernatural (1967)
28. Ryan, Alan. *Halloween Horrors* (1986)
29. Sammon, Paul M. *Splatterpunks* (two volumes) (1990)
30. Schow, David J. *Silver Scream* (1988)
31. Silva, David B. *The Best of The Horror Show* (1992)
32. Skipp, John, and Spector, Craig Spector. *Book of the Dead.* (two volumes) (1989)
33. Slung Michele. *I Shudder At Your Touch* (two volumes)(1991)
34. Tuttle, Lisa. *Skin of the Soul* (1991)
35. Wiater, Stanley. *After the Darkness* (1993)
36. Wilson, Gahan, and Collins, Nancy A. *Gahan Wilson's Ultimate Haunted House* (1996)
37. Winter, Douglas E. *Prime Evil* (1988)
38. Wolfe, Sebastian. *The Little Book of Horrors* (1992)
39. Wright, Lee and Sheehan, Richard G. *Wake Up Screaming* (1967)

About the Author

STANLEY WIATER is a widely published cineteratologist and observer of popular culture. He has interviewed more major horror and dark suspense authors, filmmakers, and artists than any other contemporary writer.

His first collection of interviews, *Dark Dreamers: Conversations with the Masters of Horror* (Avon Books, 1990), won the Bram Stoker Award for Superior Achievement from the Horror Writers Association. A companion volume, entitled *Dark Visions: Conversations with the Masters of the Horror Film* (Avon Books, 1992), was a Bram Stoker Award final ballot nominee. *Comic Book Rebels: Conversations with the Creators of the New Comics* (Donald I. Fine, 1993), co-authored with Stephen R. Bissette, was both an Eisner Award and Harvey Award nominee. A deluxe, signed edition was published by Underwood Books in 1997.

Wiater's first published short story was the sole winner of a competition judged by Stephen King. Other stories have appeared in such award-winning series as J.N. Williamson's *Masques*, Thomas F. Monteleone's *Borderlands*, and Peter Crowther's *Narrow Houses*. He has edited the acclaimed original anthologies *Night Visions 7* (Dark Harvest, 1989), and *After The Darkness* (Maclay & Associates, 1993). His work has been translated into seven languages, and in 1993 he was Master of Ceremonies at the World Horror Convention.

Wiater currently has several feature screenplays under consideration in Hollywood. His website is located at:
www.alteredearth.com/wiater/wiater.htm.
He can be e-mailed at StanWiater@aol.com.